W9-ACE-693

Praise for Emilie Griffin

Doors Into Prayer

"Superbly written . . . a marvelous reminder that prayer is a gift that God offers to everyone: One need not be a mystic or a saint to pray."
—James Martin, sj, author of *My Life with the Saints*

"Her offerings are deceptively simple and solid at the same time. Each is a gem. . . . She writes exceedingly well about what concerns and interest ordinary, busy people who also want to pray and be in relationship with God."
—*America*

"*Doors Into Prayer* is like a friendly chat about communication with and from God. . . . I would recommend this book for all adults seeking to enrich their prayer life, but especially for recent converts and young adults feeling their way into a more mature relationship with their Maker."
—*St. Anthony Messenger*

Wonderful and Dark is This Road

"A warm and inviting introduction to a subject that continues to challenge and edify both the curious and the devout."
—*Publishers Weekly*

"Griffin is a trustworthy guide to mysticism. She writes with the unmistakable authenticity and authority of a woman steeped in prayer."
—*America*

"Without reducing its wonder and power, Griffin lucidly investigates mysticism's history, its appeal and its significance as a way to knowing God. Read this beautiful book and be enlightened."
—Luci Shaw, Writer in Residence, Regent College

Emilie Griffin is a writer and editor and a native of New Orleans, Louisiana. She is the author of sixteen books on the Christian spiritual life, including *Doors Into Prayer* and *Wonderful and Dark is This Road*. She also recently collaborated with Richard Foster on a book entitled *Spiritual Classics*, and she is a contributor to the popular Advent devotional *God With Us: Rediscovering the Meaning of Christmas*. Emilie has also been active as a playwright for many years, and studied with Edward Albee at the Circle in the Square Theatre in New York City.

Emilie Griffin

Emilie Griffin

Small Surrenders

A Lenten Journey

PARACLETE PRESS
BREWSTER, MASSACHUSETTS

Small Surrenders: A Lenten Journey

2008 First Paperback Printing
2007 First Hardcover Printing

Copyright © 2007 by Emilie Griffin

ISBN: 978-1-55725-642-3

Scripture quotations are taken from the New Revised Standard
Version Bible, copyright © 1989 by the Division of Christian
Education of the National Council of the Churches of Christ
in the United States of America, and are used by permission.
All rights reserved.

The Library of Congress has catalogued the hardcover
edition as follows:

Griffin, Emilie.
    Small surrenders : a Lenten journey / Emilie Griffin.
          p. cm.
    Includes bibliographical references (p.   ).
    ISBN 978-1-55725-526-6
 1. Lent--Meditations. 2. Easter--Meditations. I. Title.
    BV85.G7155 2008
    242'.34--dc22

                                                2007034940

10 9 8 7 6 5 4 3 2 1

All rights reserved. No portion of this book may be reproduced,
stored in an electronic retreival system, or transmitted in any
form or by any means—electronic, mechanical, photocopy,
recording, or any other—except for brief quotations in printed
reviews, without the prior permission of the publisher.

Published by Paraclete Press
Brewster, Massachusetts
www.paracletepress.com
Printed in the United States of America

Contents

A Word About Lent

L ENT IN SOME SENSE IS A PLUNGE INTO A THICKET, a sustained time in a wilderness place. But few of us can put aside forty days—or forty-seven days—as a time of full retreat. Instead, we visit the wilderness without leaving our daily lives. We spend an intentional time with Jesus, entering his wilderness, walking with him, and finally, sharing his Passion. Lent is a time when we deepen our faith in a journey not of grand gestures but of small surrenders.

This book is meant to be a daily companion for the Lenten journey. Here you will find a series of reflections, one for each of the forty weekdays of Lent, the Sundays of Lent, the Easter Triduum—

those three days leading up to Easter—and Easter Sunday itself.

Since the dates of Lent and Easter vary from year to year, each selection is not for a calendar date but for a day in the Lenten season. Each meditation flows from a brief quotation on some aspect of the spiritual life. A few of these are biblical. Most are from spiritual writers and guides.

As part of your daily Lenten observance, I hope you will also read and pray the Scriptures appointed in the liturgical calendar for each day of Lent. These biblical citations (which are read aloud daily in liturgical churches) appear in three different cycles, years A, B, and C. The readings change each year, and will be repeated only every fourth year. These are the readings heard in church throughout Lent. They may also be consulted for private prayer and reflection.

These liturgical readings are found in the Roman Catholic and Anglican lectionaries, in the Common Lectionary, and on the Internet.

Externally, Lent is a time of doing without. It is a time of self-denial, a penitential time, a time of repentance. But inwardly, Lent is a time of drawing closer to Jesus. The idea is to go with Jesus into the desert and journey with him there during his times of trial. Not for one day, but for an extended time: a biblical forty days.

We begin this forty-day journey by remembering when Jesus went into the wilderness to be tempted by Satan. In fact, the Spirit drove him there. Now our task is to imitate Christ in his journey, to walk with him, to let the Spirit drive us into a desert place where Satan may confront us.

Lent is about turning: repentance and transformation. Yet we who come as practicing believers may feel that our days of conversion are already behind us. We are like the poet T.S. Eliot, who says in his poem *Ash Wednesday* that he does not want to "turn" again. To make a second or third conversion may be daunting to us. We wonder what demands the Lord will make of us during this Lenten time.

Why should we be converted again, we wonder. Aren't we Christ's people already? We are already trying to follow Jesus every day. What more is asked, then, during Lent? And why these days, these forty days?

The Church in her wisdom calls us to a special time of intentionality, still another time of repentance. Weary as we are, exhausted from the burdens of living, we must turn and be converted once again. Repentance is not a one-time thing.

T.S. Eliot speaks to my heart when he says Ash Wednesday is like climbing a staircase. We step upward slowly, prayerfully, sorry for all the ways we have gone wrong, the ways we have fallen short. We want to go up, though we're not sure where we're going, and we're rather afraid to look down.

We pray to God to have mercy on us. This is not breast-beating, but the ancient words of repentance may still reside in our memory: *Mea culpa, mea maxima culpa—through my own fault, my own most grievous fault.* Such words don't spring to our lips as they once did. Not now in the twenty-first century. We speak with a new vocabulary, the new small talk. The old phrase "ashes to ashes and dust to dust" seems a bit self-conscious, stagey. Does any of this self-denial fit with our new assertiveness, our cocky self-esteem? Yet on some level we know what flawed people we are. And if we have forgotten, Lent reminds us.

"Been to church? I see you got your ashes." *Dust we are, to dust we shall return.*

We find depth and meaning to this ritual of ashes: it is our day of departure. We are taking an inward journey, climbing with Christ along a tricky staircase, where the angle of vision continually shifts. Once again we submit to the ancient rod of discipline. God has called us to be learners, disciples, a people in training, our hearts open to change.

Lord, we want to follow you, but how will we know the way?

The forty days of Lent are counted as weekdays, Monday through Saturday. Though the Sundays are technically outside of Lent, most Lenten observance continues through the Sundays as well. In Roman Catholic and Anglican masses, purple vestments are worn on most days of Lent. The fourth Sunday of Lent has long been celebrated as *Laetare* Sunday, a day of encouragement (literally, "happy Sunday") when we look forward to Easter, two weeks away.

Today, many Protestant Christian churches are practicing Lenten observance. Even those churches that have no denominational affiliation may plan and observe Ash Wednesday as a day of repentance, and continue a special sense of spiritual dedication throughout the Lenten season. This is a sign of the Holy Spirit at work.

In earlier centuries, many Christians took on severe penances and forms of self-denial. Today's Lent is gentler and less heroic in style. The following meditations develop the theme of small surrenders, ways that we may gently open ourselves up to the grace of God.

There is no question that Lent offers an opportunity for change and transformation, especially if we join our hearts to the Lord's in the Lenten journey. As you reflect on these daily readings, I hope you will be led to experience the grace of Lent and to make your own small surrenders.

Ash Wednesday Through the First Week of Lent

Ash Wednesday

Thursday after Ash Wednesday

Friday after Ash Wednesday

Saturday after Ash Wednesday

First Sunday in Lent

Monday of the First Week

Tuesday of the First Week

Wednesday of the First Week

Thursday of the First Week

Friday of the First Week

Saturday of the First Week

Ash Wednesday

We are not converted only once in our lives but many times, and this endless series of large and small conversions, inner revolutions, leads to our transformation in Christ.

—Thomas Merton

WHAT ARE YOU GIVING UP FOR LENT?" This long-established custom of giving up treats, chocolates, caffeinated or sugary beverages, alcohol, or tobacco is perhaps the way we most often think of Lenten discipline. And it makes good conversation in casual situations. But we know it is surface stuff. Choosing to give up something good for something a bit less is a play-it-safe strategy. Something tells us there is more to spiritual transformation than this. We suspect that playing it safe is not what Christ lived and died for.

Thomas Merton's view, that we must undergo a series of large and small inner revolutions, is a truer picture of Christian transformation. When we choose some exercise for Lent, daily worship, daily prayer, abstinence from one thing or another, it is not so much the practice that transforms us. It is our willingness to change. And Merton says the process is endless. It's not about getting there, it's about being on the way.

Lent is our chance for a fresh start, a new page. We consciously let down our defenses against the grace of God. We admit to ourselves our need for improvement. We notice how hopeless we are. We tell God we're doing our best but we wish we could do better. We put ourselves in God's hands.

That is what Jesus does when he goes into the desert. He puts himself completely in God's hands. In Matthew's Gospel we read: *Then Jesus was led up by the Spirit into the wilderness to be tempted by the Devil. He fasted for forty days and forty nights, and afterwards he was famished.* (My first thought: don't try this at home.) By exposing himself to hunger Jesus opens himself up to assaults from the Devil. But he isn't just performing daredevil stunts. He makes a deliberate surrender of the will, a spiritual exercise. Jesus is placing himself in the Father's hands.

The time Jesus spends in the wilderness is a time of preparation. It is a kind of training. Jesus has a larger mission to fulfill, a ministry, a life's work. He is preparing himself for a larger call. When we go into the wilderness with Jesus our motive is similar, surrendering ourselves as a kind of preparation.

But how can we compare our little Lents to the walk Jesus takes in the wilderness? Of course the gap is huge between our holiness and his. We can hardly say our own names in his presence. But Jesus doesn't notice this gap, or he seems to overlook it.

The huge divide between our lives and his is a gap he is constantly closing. He wants us to come into the wilderness with him, if only just to observe at first. "Watch how I do this," he seems to be saying. "Notice these steps, this maneuver." Practice, he is telling us. Practice, and you'll improve, without even knowing it. Practice.

One thing we can learn from Jesus in the desert is to fortify ourselves with God's word. When the Devil tries to goad him into turning stones to bread, as a kind of power play, Jesus answers with words from Deuteronomy, Scriptures he knows by heart: It is written, *"One does not live by bread alone, but by every word that comes from the mouth of God."* The Devil wants him to break his fast. More important, he wants to weaken Jesus' allegiance.

What can we learn from just this little visit with Jesus in the wilderness? From watching him resist the Evil One?

We know, by watching Jesus, that emptiness is the beginning of holiness.

We know that we are blessed when we hunger and thirst for righteousness. We know we will be filled.

We walk with Jesus to be purified. We walk with him to be fortified. Nourished by sacrament and word, we walk through desert places more easily. We learn to deal with our own gaps, our lapses. We find that we can tolerate our hunger and our thirst.

We are converted not only once in our lives but many times. And the conversion is little by little. Sometimes it is as imperceptible as grass growing. But Lent gives us a time to move the process along. Intentionally. By small surrenders.

Merton says we "may have the generosity to undergo one or two such upheavals, (but) we cannot face the necessity of further and greater rendings of our inner self. . . ."

Merton says we cannot. But I think he knows we can. That is how our holiness grows, by small surrenders, without which we cannot finally become free.

Thursday After Ash Wednesday

Our prayer, our fasting and our almsgiving is to be done before God and not for the approval of one another—although we can give and gain support from each other in our Lenten efforts. So at home, in school, in whatever company you keep, encourage each other to mark this Lent well.

—Archbishop Vincent Nichols
Catholic Archbishop of Birmingham, England

THE SECOND DAY BEGINS TO TEACH US that Lent is a sustained experience: a true commitment to discipline. Let's go back to the question of Jesus in the desert. A one-day fast seems simple enough. But keeping a fast for forty days? It's like keeping a promise for forty days. A fast of many days can seem like a lifetime.

Still, there's a great beauty in these forty days, since we are walking toward the light. Over this sustained Lenten time the seasons will turn. Those who live in the Northern Hemisphere will move into springtime and resurrection; those who live in the Southern Hemisphere will move into autumn—and resurrection. But first we must embrace the trials and sufferings of Jesus. That is our way into the light.

How do we embrace these trials and sufferings? One good spiritual practice is to reflect on the weight of our own life choices, the constraints of living that hem us in. Possibly, instead of taking on burdens for Lent, we can be transformed by the burdens we already carry.

One of these (for some of us) is the everydayness of things. There are chores to be done, errands to perform, phone calls to return. Karl Rahner, discouraged by the daily slog, referred to his soul as a warehouse where burdens were dumped every day. Life was a hard journey of duties and obligations. This warehouse of accumulating duties was a kind of desert for him, a wilderness where he got lost and searched for the Lord. There's an irony here. Karl Rahner's relentless life of scholarship and study was entirely dedicated to the Lord's service. Yet sometimes he was overwhelmed. He lost sight of Jesus in the "warehouse" of his soul.

In our most romantic moments of conversion we wish we could drop everything to be with

Jesus, to sit at his feet, to soak up his presence. But we, too, are hemmed in by everydayness. We are tied to our work, our obligations. Jesus must come to us where we are.

Even so, in the middle of our soul's warehouse we may come to glimpse a kind of sustaining happiness. To do this we must surrender our burdens and choose a certain lightness of heart. When we choose the way of Jesus we are opting for happiness. Just one simple line in the Psalms seems to say it all: *Happy are those . . . whose hope is in the LORD their God.* If we don't follow the way of the wicked, if we avoid the attitudes of sinners, if we don't hang out with the insolent, then we will have a kind of inward happiness that keeps us going. The Psalms make a further comparison: the good person is like a tree planted near running water, yielding fruit, whose leaves never fade or fall.

Lent gives us a further chance to believe that the good and righteous person is under God's protection. And a further promise is implied in this penitential season. If we embrace godly disciplines, we will become good. And happy.

This happiness is an inward joy that no one can take away because we have chosen to serve God and to walk in his ways. God has set life and death before us. And we intend (by his grace) to choose life.

Jesus says to his disciples: *the Son of Man must undergo great suffering.* . . . Jesus has to suffer, to be rejected by the scribes and the elders, to be put to death. . . . What are our little burdens and annoyances in comparison with this?

Jesus tells us we must learn the way of self-discipline and self-denial. At the same time, he tells us not to worry, not to be anxious, not to be afraid. To accept our lives with all their constraints, for Jesus' sake, is a small surrender. That is one way we can follow Jesus and take up the cross.

Friday After Ash Wednesday

Why then has this people turned away in perpetual backsliding?

—Jeremiah

IN LENT A DISOBEDIENT PEOPLE RETURNS to God and is reconciled to him. That disobedience is what Jeremiah and the other prophets were constantly lamenting. Why would a people so cherished by God, so favored by his presence and his love, be always drifting away? As we move into Lent, we might well take Jeremiah's question for granted, admitting in principle that we are backsliders, but going no farther. We can move from his question to the next one: how, exactly, are we backsliding? What is it that we have failed to do? Or believe?

For many of us the constant onslaught of errands and duties may pile up until it becomes a wall between us and God. We do not consciously turn away from God. Instead, we drift away, like ships without rudders, with no particular aim in mind.

Therefore one thing we can do in Lent is to make a deliberate return. Here the context from

Jeremiah may help. In Jeremiah the prophet (speaking for God) is upset because people have turned away to serve false gods. They have allowed even the temple to be overrun by these alien deities. Maybe Jeremiah gives us a clue for our own self-examination. Have we become insensitive to God's commands? Have we become forgetful of the presence of God within us and around us?

Over the centuries Christians have developed checklists for examining our hearts. The Seven Deadly Sins are one such checklist. Usually they are given as pride, envy, anger, laziness, greed, gluttony, and lust. Is one or more of these getting in the way of our fidelity to God? One good way to reflect on these deadly sins is to think of a positive quality that is the opposite of each of the sins mentioned. For example, the opposite of pride is humility, or maybe modesty or simplicity. Can we consciously embrace one of these virtues? That is one way to distance ourselves from one or more of the deadly sins.

Another good way to examine our hearts is to reflect on the Ten Commandments. These spiritual commands can become a scheme for reflection, a way of detecting our own strengths and weaknesses. *Have no other Gods before me. Do not worship false gods. Do not steal. Do not commit murder. Do not commit adultery. Do not misuse God's name. Do not lie, especially not under oath. Do not covet your neighbor's wife (husband) goods, servants, or home. Keep the Sabbath holy. Honor your father and your mother.*

Still another framework for righteousness is found in the Beatitudes. Jesus praises those who are meek, pure of heart, poor, or poor in spirit, as well as those who are reviled and persecuted for righteousness' sake. Jesus holds up for admiration those who have made both large and small surrenders. They are not mighty and powerful, but simple and faithful. Because of this, the Beatitudes may give us insight into our own need for surrender.

Some of us have memorized both the Ten Commandments and the Beatitudes, and that is a fine thing to do. But we should beware of considering these as merely a set of moral teachings. They are clues to the wisdom of God implanted in the faithful soul. Often our self-righteousness prevents us from hearing what God wants to say to us. A powerful event, a disgrace, a humiliation may be needed before we can actually listen to God.

Consider the story of Charles Colson, who was special counsel to President Nixon at the time of the Watergate scandals. Charles Colson was not a nice person. He subscribed to the widely held view that nice guys finish last.

At that time in his life Charles Colson was not likely to sit down and reflect on the Beatitudes or the Ten Commandments. He was too far from God for that. Instead, his wall of separation from God was punctured by the intervention of a friend. Tom Phillips, the CEO of a major company, was someone who really cared about Colson. At a critical moment, when Colson was down and out, Tom Phillips spoke to Colson about friendship with Christ. Then and there, he gave Colson a copy of *Mere Christianity*, and read aloud to him the chapter on pride and conceit.

At first, Charles Colson kept up his wall of resistance, but at last he gave in. He longed to be an honest man again, so much so that in his Watergate testimony he went beyond his legal obligations. He was more honest than the law required, and he went to prison for what he admitted to having done. He lost his freedom because he was sent to prison, and he lost his livelihood because he could no longer practice law. Yet, his time in prison was part of his surrender. He began praying with his fellow prisoners. And when he was released from prison, he established a prison ministry. He learned a new way to live.

Colson's surrender was a major, life-changing event. Perhaps what God is asking of us right now is smaller: a small surrender. But have we put even a small transformation out of our minds? Have we turned away? Have we stopped taking God at his word, or thinking of ourselves in terms of his covenant of love?

I suspect that we are always drifting, putting space between God and ourselves. John Henry Newman says, "We are ever but beginning. . . . The most perfect Christian is to himself but a beginner, a penitent prodigal, who has squandered God's gifts, and comes to him to be tried over again, not as a son, but as a hired servant." This beginning again, this surrender, is one way to start living the Beatitudes.

Saturday After Ash Wednesday

If grace is so wonderful, why do we have such difficulty recognizing and accepting it? Maybe it's because grace is not gentle or made-to-order. It often comes disguised as loss, or failure, or unwelcome change.

—Kathleen Norris

AS A YOUNG WOMAN I WENT TO NEW YORK City looking for a job. Becoming rather desperate when the pickings were lean, I went into a church and prayed for a job. Amazingly, I got a job offer within twenty-four hours.

But though I took the job, I did not receive it as a grace. "Oh, that couldn't have been an answer to prayer," I told myself. The answer, if answer it was, had been so swift, so forthcoming, that I refused to receive it as such. "It would have happened anyway," I thought. I accused myself of superstitious thinking and went on my way.

Within a week or so my new employer, who was not a particularly religious man, organized an office lunch at a nearby restaurant. While all of us were chatting he suddenly said, "Have you ever noticed how often people pray for things, and then they forget to thank God for the things they receive in prayer?" The environment could not have been more un-churchy, more secular. I can't even remember how the topic came up.

But (as it then seemed) God had gotten my attention in this odd sort of way. And slowly I began to suspect that there are graces bombarding us daily, like unseen radio waves, but we are not fully tuned in. This is one way we make a surrender. We admit that God may be speaking to us through the most casual and ordinary events of our lives.

In my own pilgrimage toward God I began to realize the value of attentiveness. It was important to interpret small events in the light of God's grace and mercy. This in itself was a small surrender. It is one I have continued to make, not only in my first acceptance of God, but over and over again.

There are so many examples of this need for a willing attentiveness to God's grace.

Take the story of Avery Dulles who, as a student at Harvard, struggled with large philosophical questions. One day when he had been cooped up in the Widener Library, reading Augustine's book *The City of God*, he went out for a breath of fresh air and walked along the bank of the nearby Charles River. There he saw a young tree just starting to bud. And what he noticed was the tree's obedience. The tree had not invented its own life story. It was following a path set by a greater being. Suddenly Dulles got it: the existence of God, the intelligence, the goodness, the benevolence.

Later that night, in his room, Dulles tried to pray. It had been so long since he'd prayed, he couldn't remember all the words of the Lord's Prayer. But slowly the words came back to him.

Not every story of grace is so sweet and tender. John of the Cross, one of our deepest teachers of prayer, was seized and imprisoned by his fellow religious. But because he was attentive to grace, he felt God's presence, even in a sixteenth-century prison cell where his body was cramped and twisted.

John of the Cross had no pencil or paper. But in that terrible circumstance he was attentive to God and was able to see the grace in a harsh situation. In his prison cell he composed a poem that became a treasure of the spiritual life: "One dark night," it begins. That poem, which he later wrote down after he was set free, became one of the great texts on prayer, yielding the notion of the "dark night of the soul."

So, as Kathleen Norris says, grace is not always gentle or made to order. Unpleasant times, such as getting stuck overnight in an airport and having to sleep in a chair, can become not just moments of misery but also times of understanding and reflection.

Norris wants us to find the hidden grace in negative situations, in crisis, in emergency, in loss. She interprets the hideous events of September 11, 2001, seeing the power of human love, the cell phone calls, the tender goodbyes, the expressions of friendship, even the brief solidarity and unity that Americans and their sympathizers felt.

With a keen eye for grace, Kathleen Norris wants us to sharpen our vision, our hearing, our gift of interpretation.

This is a small surrender. But if we make it, God can speak to us. Over and over again. In the most unlikely ways.

First Sunday in Lent

"You see, the older I get, the more I ask myself, 'How is my life unfolding in terms of my primary goal of living with God forever?'"

—Brennan Manning

Some of us never ask how our life is unfolding with regard to God. Those of us who do ask this question may not ask it very often. We are almost afraid to wonder how we are doing because we suspect we are not doing very well.

One of the best things about Lent is that it takes us out of the routine of the year and raises the great spiritual questions. My first formal instruction in the Christian life included this admonition: "A Lent missed is a year lost from the spiritual life." The priest who made that statement probably considered it to be commonplace. But to me it was a stark novelty. *Is Lent that important?* I found myself asking. Is Lent an essential passage in the spiritual progress of the year? It was a breakthrough idea that continues to shape the spiritual life for me.

Yes, Lent has been marked out by the church as a time to ask oneself the big questions: What am I doing with my time? What am I doing with my life? How well am I expressing the imprint of Christ upon my heart? How deep is my charity? How deep is my love? How devoted is my service? How is my life unfolding in terms of my primary goal of living with God forever?

You could say that Lent is a time of benchmarks. And the big question is, how well am I functioning in the Christian life? Am I living sacrificially? Am I living for others? Do I have God's love completely overflowing in my life, so plentiful that I want to share it and give it away?

Often we think our obligation as Christians is to evangelize, to spread the good news, to bring others to Christ. Yes, that is true. But the most incisive way to do that is to become a "little Christ," to become like Christ in such a beguiling way that others are deeply attracted by God's life in us.

Am I cheerful? Do I find a moment of brightness in the day? Can I respond to someone else's need, not in a showy way, but just because, when the moment presents itself, I do or say the right thing? Reviewing our days with this kind of mini-evaluation is good Lenten discipline.

And then there is maxi-evaluation, the mega-evaluation, looking for the big picture. What large-scale venture have I undertaken to express my Christian love? How have I given a good example? How have I counseled? How have I witnessed? How have I served?

That's Lent. It's a time of coming back to the question, how well am I doing? How is my life unfolding in terms of my primary goal of living with God forever?

Sometimes, an accurate answer to that question eludes us. That's where spiritual friendship (or spiritual direction) comes in.

The fact is, we are often hard on ourselves. We take note of all the ways we fall short, but we fail to notice the ways we have been pleasing to God. Spiritual friends (who love us with a godly love) can give us a more accurate picture. That's why friendship, godly friendship, is one of the ways we can and should pursue the spiritual life. Authentic friends will tell us honestly where we have fallen short. But they will also tell us not to beat up on ourselves. And they will remind us of our good deeds and good dispositions.

Spiritual friends will help us to live for God daily, hourly. This is is rarely a question of grandiose gestures. More often what we need are small adjustments in the management of our time, our attitudes, our behavior. Friends can help us to gain perspective, to make modest surrenders.

This kind of attitude adjustment is in fact a form of spiritual formation and transformation. It is not showy, it is not self-righteous, it is not flashy. It is a way of living well and making good choices that does not aspire to fame.

Ideally, we should be asking ourselves these tough spiritual questions throughout the year. But Lent is a special time for yielding to the grace of God. There is no time like the present to ask how we are doing, and to notice the Lenten benchmarks.

Monday of the First Week

What then are we to say? Should we continue in sin in order that grace may abound? By no means! How can we who died to sin go on living in it?

—Letter of Paul to the Romans

SOMETIMES I THINK MOST OF US HAVE forgotten what sin means. Words like "sin" and "transgression" may sound oddly archaic. We have even lost the sense of sin. Why is it hard to think of ourselves as sinners? Possibly it is because we have lost hope.

On the news every day we hear a long recitation of the sins of our fellow humans. We hear of managers of companies who have stolen the lifelong savings of their investors, without any possible restitution. We hear stories of people who have kidnapped other people's children and have possibly raped and killed them. Violent, lawless behavior is everywhere, and only a fraction of it can be excused by mental illness or somehow explained away. We see images of soldiers, who were trained to protect us or quell the violence in societies, who have taken matters into their own hands and gunned down innocent bystanders. We hear of dictators who have destroyed not only their enemies but members of their own societies, crushing the life out of their own people to maintain order and submission: Joseph Stalin, Adolf Hitler, Pol Pot, Saddam Hussein.

To regard the sins of others may be horrifying. But it is far worse to know what our own sins are. Even worse than our sins, which can be forgiven if we admit them and express contrition, is our tendency to sin. An ugly sea of possible wrongdoing surges within us. Augustine of Hippo calls this "concupiscence," a word that suggests not only sexual sin: it means our human weakness across the board.

There is only one remedy for this continual turning away from God. It is simply a matter of turning back, conversion, *metanoia*. In the Gospel of Mark we read that John the Baptist came preaching a gospel of repentance. After him came an even greater prophet, Jesus of Nazareth, who called us to repent: "Repent and believe in the good news."

The good news is that sin has no ultimate power over us if we give ourselves to God. Sometimes it seems that forty days would not be long enough to let this truth soak in. If we spent the whole of Lent believing in the good news of Jesus, we still could not fully absorb this boundless treasure.

One way to spend Lent, even as we reflect on our sins, is to consciously dwell on our redemption. No, the glass is not half empty. It is half full. The full half is the important half, the part that can make our lives complete and whole.

The more we know we have been rescued and redeemed, the less we are likely to stumble and fall. To be sure, our humanity is flawed, and will remain so. But Jesus has our lives in hand, and we are continually on the mend.

A blizzard of grace is hovering over us, blanketing our transgressions and hiding the ugliness we're so ashamed of. Maybe it is not so much winter as spring. Grace is pushing shoots up, buds are swelling, joy is trying hard to bloom.

If Jesus Christ has done everything to redeem us, do we have to do anything? Well, yes. We have to accept the possibility of our own transformation.

We have to receive the grace, interpret the grace, name the grace. We have to act according to the grace we have received; we have to incarnate the message. We have to let ourselves become surprised by joy.

All the old theological debates can be put aside while we absorb this reality. Jesus has stemmed the tide of sin for us and has stood in the gap for us: this truth will pervade us if we let it.

This lovely fact of what Jesus has done for us through grace evokes a response from us: we choose to do good deeds during Lent. And such an organized scheme of good behavior, even just a few weeks of it, could possibly reshape us, remake our habits, and help us to love the good. Possibly we will come to recognize more clearly what is good, and what goodness we are capable of.

We dwell on our redemption when we take on small acts of goodness: A letter to a friend. A visit to someone who is ill. Hours of service donated in a worthy cause. Extra time spent with a child, offering an outing or a special treat.

In short, we can use our Lenten time to shift awareness from sin to reconciliation. Jesus has reconciled us to the Father. Now we can reimagine our own lives in terms of reconciliation. What quarrels could we mend? What old enemies can we forgive? Are there grudges in our hearts that need to be shed?

By every small choice we make for good—by every small surrender—we are reaching toward our transformation. By consciously choosing the life of grace, we find that other things will start to come right. This transformation doesn't happen all at once. Instead, grace comes little by little. But we can choose. We begin to grasp by experience what we read in Galatians: "It is no longer I who live, but it is Christ who lives in me. And the life I now live in the flesh I live by faith in the Son of God."

*Do not judge, and you will not be judged; do not condemn,
and you will not be condemned. Forgive, and you will be
forgiven; give, and it will be given to you.*

—Luke

ONE WAY TO APPROACH LENT IS TO TRY
to discover our worst flaws and work on
these—to surrender, if you will, our worst character failings. An example of this is told by
Catherine Marshall, who considered herself
to be too critical of others. She gave herself a
task to fast from critical remarks for one day, and
she found this very difficult. More and more she
became convinced that condemnation was one of
her worst flaws. Also she scolded herself for being
highly opinionated about politics, government,
and people in public life. (How would today's
news media fare if they tried to live by Catherine
Marshall's standards?)

Recently, in a book group, we held a heated
discussion about Marshall's self-imposed "fast

from criticalness." Some participants thought that critical judgment is not a failing, and that Marshall was putting herself through the wringer to no good purpose. Point taken. But does that mean that Jesus' instruction "Do not judge" is not such a great idea? Is he right to say we should not condemn?

When Jesus says, "Do not judge," he is not discouraging us from reasoned critical evaluations. Instead, he is warning us against heaping blame on others. Jesus lived in a religious culture that brought harsh judgments against sinners. Sinners were outcasts, and some were stoned to death. Religious conformity was demanded, and those who deviated from the norm endured harsh religious judgments. Jesus wanted to encourage a spirit of forgiveness and tolerance even towards those who had broken the rules. He did not condone their sins, but neither did he condone harsh judgment against them.

Is it important, then, to get to work on our worst sins and try to sandpaper them away? In past times those pursuing a life of virtue might have made notes on every one of their failings and falls from grace within a twenty-four-hour period. Though this spot-checking has a long history, this kind of self-criticism may not be a good idea. Such a blame game—even against ourselves—seems based on a narrow understanding of God as a vindictive Being who is pointing his finger at us and keeping track of whatever we do wrong.

In several parables, Jesus shows us a God who goes out of his way to forgive. The parable of the workers in the vineyard is a fine portrayal of God's generous forgiveness and mercy. Jesus compares God to a vineyard keeper who pays the same wages to workers who sign on late as to those who have been toiling through the heat of the day.

Can we accept the idea of a God who is so merciful, so forgiving? Whose justice is so mysterious, so hard to decipher by ordinary rules?

For some of us, this is difficult to accept. But I think the best way to let go of our own judgmentalism is to remember the boundless mercy of God. Rather than make a list of our own slips, rather than chronicle our own self-righteousness, we should let go even of judging ourselves.

Instead, we should focus on the immeasurable love of God. To remember how deeply God loves us is to feel that we have love to give back, to others and to God.

When we ourselves are struggling for a larger vision of God, when we want to expand our vision of God's mercy, one way we can do so is through stories told by modern writers in which God reaches out to hopelessly troubled sinners. Graham Greene is such a writer, one who may have seen himself as beyond the boundaries of grace. In Greene's world, sometimes called "Greeneland," we find a landscape of ambiguity and loss in which God is portrayed as mysteriously constant and faithful, even to those who have doubted and fled from him.

In Greene's stories God's mercy is extended to spiritual lepers, those whose lives are infected with doubt, addiction, atheism, and despair. The mystery is that God does not let go of them, does not reject them. By showing God as present to these modern outcasts and transgressors, Greene's writing enlarges our vision of God.

Greene's view of a loving God is not a license to steal or transgress. It's more like a modern version of Jesus healing the lepers when no one else would come near them. It's like Jesus dining with tax collectors and sinners when others kept them at arm's length.

How do we let go of judgmentalism? Not by our own efforts, but by surrendering to God's grace. Not by knowing everything, but by knowing more and more about the mystery of God's forgiveness and love.

Wednesday of the First Week

I . . . don't always have wonderful thoughts or feelings when I pray. . . . But I believe that something is happening because God is greater than my mind and heart. The larger mystery of prayer is greater than what I can grasp.

—Henri Nouwen

WHEN I FIRST BEGAN TO BE SERIOUS ABOUT prayer, I began to see prayer as a landscape, an undiscovered country, a universe. Without knowing much about prayer I had entered into contemplation and gained what are known sometimes as "beginner's pleasures" or "beginner's consolations." I felt wonderful when I prayed and wanted to pray more and more.

But after some weeks these joys and consolations vanished without a trace. I was mystified, and at first I tried to re-create my first experiences. But I simply could not. Soon I began to appreciate what many of the great writers say about prayer. Prayer is a mystery, an adventure, an experience that cannot be easily catalogued or pinned down.

We cannot dictate beforehand how prayer will affect us or how we will feel. We must simply surrender our expectations and pray.

The best spiritual teachers tell us our prayer should not depend on feelings. Ignatius Loyola speaks about desolation and consolation as a kind of inevitable see-saw effect in the spiritual life. Desolation follows consolation; consolation follows desolation. Sometimes there are middling experiences when we have no idea what is going on.

But we continue to pray. That is faithfulness. And if we make a sustained effort at prayer—five minutes, ten minutes, fifteen, or even longer—some kind of grace is given to us. We may not have clarity. We may not have feelings of exaltation. But God is with us. We are living in grace.

Ideally, we should not think, when we have consolations and joys, that our prayer has been successful; on the other hand, we should not think that when our prayer is desolate, it has somehow been a waste of time. It's best to accept the variations and mood swings of prayer as part of what God has in mind for us. Praying is not about our competence. It is about grace.

At last I came to an appreciation that prayer (any kind of extended prayer) is influenced by moods and seasons. I began to describe these, sketching them out, as it were, picturing the prayer landscape. I named these aspects of prayer life, not using the old language I had received, but using words of my own. Here are some words that I learned to use:

"Beginning" is the return we make to the Lord whenever we overcome our resistance and pray. "Yielding" is the surrender we make when we fully give way to the prayer experience, yielding up our former opinions and attitudes and allowing God to speak to us in new ways.

"Darkness" is the sense we sometimes have of being stuck in a wilderness without clear tracks or directions. Henri Nouwen alludes to this mood of alienation: "I . . . don't always have wonderful thoughts or feelings when I pray. . . . But I believe that something is happening because God is greater than my mind and heart. The larger mystery of prayer is greater than what I can grasp."

There is still another mood of prayer I call "transparency," the exalted phase in which everything seems lighted up from within. Sometimes, when prayer is consoling, we sense a deeper vision, a greater depth of field. Again, we should not hold onto this. Blessings like these should wash over us like a light summer rain.

"Fear of heights" is that mood in which we begin to know we are advancing in prayer, and we are afraid that God may give us a greater challenge than we can handle. In fact, this is an aspect of doubt, or a lack of trust in God's purpose for our lives, but it comes as a regular mood in prayer.

Because prayer is not entirely solitary, but it is rather an aspect of our spiritual friendships, I also included spiritual friendship as a mood of prayer, to signify the binding power of grace. Here I borrowed a line from Shakespeare and called this binding power "hoops of steel."

Finally, I called the seventh mood "clinging." Clinging is also my overarching metaphor for prayer. By this I mean a mutual clinging, in which the Lord holds onto us and we to him, when we put our whole reliance on him.

I say that these were my own words, but in fact, they came to me through the experience of prayer and through discernment. The term "clinging" is used by Augustine of Hippo and by Thomas Aquinas, and more recently by Karl Rahner. And the Hebrew mystics, I am told, use the word *devekut* to describe intimacy with God; this Hebrew word is best rendered in English as "clinging." There is nothing really original in the spiritual life. All this discernment of grace comes to us from the ancient Jewish and Christian experience of prayer.

It is useful, I think, to know that we are praying in a long tradition, and that others from all the centuries are with us in our prayer. At the same time, what is important is not so much to know about prayer as to pray.

Thursday of the First Week

If you cannot go into the desert, you must nonetheless "make some desert" in your life. Every now and then leaving . . . and looking for solitude to restore, in prolonged silence and prayer, the stuff of your soul.

—Carlo Carretto

WHEN I BEGAN THE SPIRITUAL LIFE IN earnest I was living and working in New York City, tending a marriage, raising young children, managing a household, and handling a full-time job in a very worldly, that is to say secular, situation.

Yes, it was possible to pray (briefly) in the middle of daily life, in the kitchen, in the playroom, in the grocery store, while running errands in the car. I did that as well as I could. But there was a deeper kind of prayer I could not manage in the craziness of daily affairs without reaching for "desert times."

Many churches in New York City keep their doors open for prayer throughout the day and into the evening. Sometimes I could slip in and pause for intense times of silence, solitude, and prayer. Imagination can help us to find "desert spaces" in the middle of our many activities. Is it possible to get up early before the household is awake? Or to stay up later than others to find a desert time? Churches are not always open, but one can begin to look for and identify sacred places.

Possibly the "desert" is in the blank page of a journal, a page so dry and unwelcoming that it gives us a full, thirsty experience of desolation. We seem to be walking barefoot through the sand of empty pages, because our souls are dry and we have nothing to say.

One way to go into the desert is by entering into the darkest spaces of daily life: long stretches when the subway runs under the East River, or the PATH train glides under the Hudson; in the long hideous tangle of a traffic jam; waiting at the department of motor vehicles in a line that won't move. We can call these times of annoyance and frustration, or we can embrace them, these black holes of uncertainty, as God-given desert time.

What can we learn about surrender from Carlo Carretto? This dedicated social activist led the

Italian youth movement of Catholic Action for twenty years. But at midlife he wanted more. Carretto went, literally, into the African desert to join the Little Brothers of Jesus in the deserts of North Africa. He saw this as following a call from God. "Leave everything and come with me. . . ." The letters he sent back were eventually published as *Letters from the Desert,* and he became a world-renowned voice for a kind of desert spirituality that many could embrace.

To enter the desert, Carretto knew, is an act of the religious imagination. Some can enter the desert without leaving home. Others, less sensitive, less imaginative, have to feel the sand and the burning heat.

Carretto was plunged into the spiritual life. He understood the dryness of prayer firsthand. When he read classic texts such as *The Cloud of Unknowing* or the writings of John of the Cross, these mystical books made sense to him because he had been to the desert himself. They were describing a necessary passage in the life of the spirit.

Carretto says that we may enter the desert through exhaustion. Instead of being able to imagine our way in, we find that our imagination has run out. We are tired, we are worn out, we don't know how to pray or what to make of what God is saying—or isn't saying.

These are true desert experiences. They are not romantic. They are not always dramatic. Sometimes they are dull and dry. These are the desert experiences we don't plan. Yet we can receive them. Rather than ignoring them and wishing they would go away, we can consciously receive them as a work of grace.

"What is this dryness in meditation which I am describing, this refusal to fix our thoughts on spiritual things?" Carretto helps us to interpret the dryness, and won't let us feel overconfident. "Difficulty in meditation is not always the sign of an advance of the soul towards God, or the progress to a higher sort of prayer. But it may, thank God, be a sign of that."

Carretto cautions us to seek good guidance when we interpret the movements of the spirit. But he also says that when we just crave the emptiness and silence of sitting at the feet of God in an act of love, it means something. "It means

something great. It is one of the most beautiful
secrets of the spiritual life."

We are responsible for our own solitude. Precisely because our secular milieu offers us so few spiritual disciplines, we have to develop our own.

—Henri Nouwen

SOLITUDE IS A HUMAN NEED, A NEED FOR everyone. Never mind about who is an extrovert or an introvert. Solitude offers an opportunity for reflection, for sorting things out. There are days when I feel driven out of the workplace (simply because it is the workplace) into another place: a coffeehouse, a bench outdoors, a porch swing, a chair in the library. Such places, as much as a church pew, provide openings to grace.

How do we use this solitude? For me, at first, this time is no more than a straightening up process. I open my briefcase to find countless jumbled papers: receipts, odd assortments of cash and coin, appointment slips, ticket stubs, a worn calendar, a half-filled notebook, a pen and pencil case, a cell phone. The state of the briefcase reveals the chaos of my life, my state of mind. I'd better turn the cell phone off, for now. It is time, in the middle of everything, to come into quiet as best I can.

Sometimes in workshops on prayer I hear questions (often from those who are just beginning) about how to design a structure for spiritual life. Obviously, there are many ways to answer them. When talking to a group of young mothers not long ago, I did not mention solitude as primary, lest that sound too monastic, too far out of reach. Instead, I emphasized keeping a journal. By this I meant a dedicated journal, reserved for reporting on our spiritual encounters. "How do you go about this? Well, you make a trip to the drug store, you choose an inexpensive composition book, a pen that you like. . . ." By the ordinariness of my response, I wanted to make the spiritual life practical and accessible. "It's not so hard; just try it."

But a journal only appears to be ordinary. In fact, it may open an extraordinary path. The journal's empty pages become a way into solitude. They invite recollection, or centering. We stare at the blank pages, trying to bring ourselves into stillness. We empty our hearts and minds of the trivial, the distracting, the annoying details.

After clearing a space for God we may begin our conversation with God. This is an act of the religious imagination, but it is also part of the sorting-out process. In front of the Lord, we pull out our unfinished agendas, our unfulfilled desires, our unrequited loves. *What is to be done about this?* We want to know. Depending on the level of our need, we may find ourselves shouting out our complaints to God. We tell him what is lacking. We point out what injustices are making us angry. We tell God what is wrong and ask him to award us damages.

Once we have done this—voiced our complaints to God—something vital has happened. We are occupying a new sort of space, a space in the presence of God. That in itself is prayer. Even if our end of the conversation is wailing, whining, and negative, still, we have opened a door into prayer. This is the actual entrance into prayer, following a time-honored dictum: put yourself into the presence of God. When we have made space, done our sorting, and voiced even our smallest questions, we are praying. Interrogation is prayer. Negotiation is prayer. In the same way, stillness in the presence of God, a listening attitude, is also prayer.

Henri Nouwen writes, "We are responsible for our own solitude." Solitude is one way we imitate Jesus, who went apart for times of solitude even though his life was already filled with prayer. Early in the morning, while it was still dark, he went outside into a solitary place for prayer. Besides that, Jesus spent forty days fasting in the desert as a preparation for his ministry.

The poet Kay Ryan says, in her poem "Shark's Teeth," that "Everything contains some silence." She writes as though rest could be measured in small shark's tooth fragments angled inside our noise. This is a poet's construct, but it is somehow true. When I am in the coffeehouse, with my journal open on the table, I am surrounded by noise: coffeehouse workers taking orders from customers and joking with each other, recorded music playing over a loudspeaker, muffled conversation at nearby tables, traffic outside. But Ryan imagines that an hour in the city somehow holds within it "remnants of a time when silence reigned. . . ." I think she is right. Like the ancients, she harks back to a forgotten time, an age of gold, a silence that governed everything.

Is this a holy silence? Ryan doesn't say so, and maybe she isn't sure. But Christians believe the voice of God permeates the universe and can be heard if only we slow down and tune into the place where silence reigns.

Saturday of the First Week

Yet even now, says the LORD, return to me with all your heart, with fasting, with weeping, and with mourning; rend your hearts and not your clothing. Return to the LORD, your God, for he is gracious and merciful, slow to anger, and abounding in steadfast love, and relents from punishing.

—Joel

WHAT DOES IT MEAN TO RETURN TO THE Lord? In reality, this is something we need to do almost on a daily basis. Lent simply heightens this necessity and turns a glaring light on our casual indifference.

Is it a long stretch to see our relationship to God as a romantic love story? Possibly we resist such a comparison, thinking it sentimental or contrived. But the Bible (especially the Song of Songs) makes this comparison readily. The Lord comes to us as a lover. Christ is represented as a bridegroom, and we in the church are his bride. Great mystical writers such as Bernard of Clairvaux and John of the Cross make similar comparisons.

Do we resist the notion that God is court-
ing us? Bede Griffiths, a well-known British
Benedictine monk, relates his conversion in
his book *The Golden String.* In this narrative he
is constantly guided by the voice of God and
drawn more and more to repentance: "I felt an
overwhelming need to repent. I did not clearly
understand what repentance was, nor was I aware
of any particular sin of which I had to repent."
Instead, Griffiths was dealing with unrest in
his soul. He had moved from discontent with
the world to a discontent with himself. And he
says this desire for repentance "came to me as a
command, and I kept saying to myself, scarcely
knowing the meaning of what I said, 'I must
repent, I must repent.'"

This powerful movement of the spirit led
Griffiths to spend an entire night in prayer.
Admittedly, he was given to extravagant gestures. Still, he felt a powerful summons and tried
to figure out how to respond. "Again," he says,
"the resolution seemed to come not of my own
volition; it was an instinct with the force of a
command."

Yet, when Griffiths tried to sustain an all-night prayer vigil, his soul was filled with conflicts. What an absurd, foolish thing he was attempting to do, he thought. How ridiculous he must appear to other people! He felt silly and self-conscious. He feared some irrationality at work in him, something he was unable to control. He began to be afraid of isolation, of being different and behaving differently from everyone else.

Yet he felt a call from God, one he could not ignore. Of this struggle he said: "I do not wish to exaggerate the nature of this ordeal, but it was indeed the turning-point of my life." Griffiths felt called to surrender himself to a God he could not understand, Someone above his reason who expected him to trust and obey. Eventually the only way he was able to handle this experience was by placing himself with Christ in Gethsemane, and waiting for the night to pass.

He got through the night this way, but in the morning felt exhausted and without consolation. Then again the voice came into his mind: "You must go to a retreat." What an amazing word! But Griffiths had never made a retreat and did not even know what a retreat was. He could only suppose it was some kind of "clerical conference taking place in the country."

But he went, obediently, to a nearby Anglo-Catholic church and asked about retreats. Surprisingly, he learned that a retreat was beginning that morning, one that he would be welcome to join. In the retreat Griffiths learned about such teachings as the Incarnation and the Trinity in ways he had never heard them taught before.

So in this way, young Griffiths experienced the fullness of repentance, not a mere expression of sorrow for small transgressions, but the full gift of himself to God.

What about us? Are we likely to have such remarkable experiences ourselves? Or do they come only to certain individuals at peak moments in a lifetime? No doubt we struggle against the high drama of God's love. But in tenderness and compassion, he is pursuing us all the same.

Second Sunday Through the Second Week of Lent

Second Sunday in Lent

Monday of the Second Week

Tuesday of the Second Week

Wednesday of the Second Week

Thursday of the Second Week

Friday of the Second Week

Saturday of the Second Week

Second Sunday in Lent

Every walk is a story, a narrative line leading out from home to a point of crisis, change or insight and then back to the known and a time of reflection.

—John Leax

SIX WEEKS IS ONLY A SMALL SLICE OF THE YEAR. But the six weeks of Lent, forty days and the Sundays, give us a chance to look at the story—the full narrative sweep—of our lives with God. As we look at the narrative of Jesus, we look at our own lives, and we renew our desire to walk beside Jesus all along the way, following his way in our own journeys.

How in fact is this narrative, this combined and intertwined story, moving along?

Let's look first at the Jesus story. We could say that Jesus settled quite young on his life task. When he was twelve years old he was already instructing his elders on the deeper meanings of Scripture. His parents were amazed at his gifts and his audacity.

But much of his early life story is hidden from us. Only when he takes up his public ministry do we see the trajectory clearly. Jesus goes into the desert to prepare himself. He stays in the desert and makes a long fast. There he is tempted by Satan and successfully resists. Later, Jesus seeks baptism from John, in the Jordan. Jesus begins to gather a group of disciples, a team, if you will. Jesus goes from town to town preaching and teaching, telling stories and healing, and offering certain signs. Word spreads. His ministry grows unmanageably large. Multitudes gather. Pressure mounts. Authorities become nervous. Finally, there is the entrance into Jerusalem, and the events leading up to his passion and death.

Well, that is the capsule summary. Just a sketch really, for we know the narrative is much larger. But now let's look at our own narratives in the light of his.

When we start to measure our lives by Jesus' life, immediately we fall short. And we see how even our attempt to grasp his story is inadequate. What is it in the Jesus story that really matters to us? What can we imitate in our own lives? We are not called to do exactly what Jesus did, go where he went, or say what he said. It is how he lived, the love and power he radiated, his sacrificial love and concern for each person that we most want to imitate.

We notice the love of Jesus in many of the healings he performed. The man with the withered hand. The woman with the flow of blood. Jairus's daughter. The centurion's daughter. Simon's mother who was not feeling well when Jesus came to stay. His friend Lazarus, whom he raised from the dead when Lazarus had already been in the tomb four days.

We notice the love of Jesus in the way he related to people, especially the people most often shunned by the righteous. We notice him eating and drinking, visiting with tax collectors and sinners. We notice him speaking with the Samaritan woman at the well. We remember how he forgave the woman taken in adultery, and saved her from being stoned to death. We see the way he treated the woman who came to anoint him with perfume in an alabaster jar.

And then we see how he loved children: "Allow the little children to come to me," Jesus said. He is often pictured this way, with children scrambling around to talk to him.

In all these ways Jesus showed his love.

The poet John Leax says that every narrative is a line leading out to a point of crisis, change, or insight and then back to the known and a time of reflection. What Leax gives us is a way to distill the meaning of a story by looking for a point of crisis, a turning point. The Jesus story has turning points. Obviously Jesus has a purpose in his time on earth, one that he pursues with eagerness and dedication. Because he is God we suspect that he knows the future better than we do. But Jesus acts as a man, one who waits for the Father's insight and clarification. Jesus knows, and he doesn't know. Even so, in all his dealings he lives his story with wisdom, compassion, and love.

Our own narratives have turning points as well. Over and over again we make choices. When we come to moments of insight and reflection, we have an opportunity to choose the way of Jesus again, even if we have already chosen his way of love. Conversion is not just a quick, once-and-for-all moment of insight and change. Conversion is a lifelong story, a long-range focusing and refocusing, a constantly renewed fidelity.

It may be that Lent, this particular Lent, is a chance to make a certain choice over again. In our own stories we may find some issue, long festering, that can come into healing and forgiveness at last. Perhaps the main insight will be as simple as this: my story is linked eternally to the Jesus story. And I will walk with him to the end.

Monday of the Second Week

God whispers to us in our pleasures, speaks in our conscience, but shouts in our pains. It is His megaphone to arouse a deaf world.

—C. S. Lewis

PART OF THE ANCIENT LANGUAGE OF THE spiritual life is purgation, or the purgative way. Our sorrows and our pains are supposedly good for us. They provide a kind of brushing up, a cleansing, a burnishing. In Scripture we hear a lot about the way we can be improved by adversity. Frankly, this concept may hang together theologically, but it is hard to accept when you are the one in adverse circumstances.

C.S. Lewis wrote books to answer his own most baffling questions. In *The Problem of Pain* he tries to decipher the meaning of pain, to reconcile the idea of a good God with the seemingly merciless character of pain. Pain, he suggests, is God's megaphone to arouse a deaf world.

Lewis represents himself, and each one of us, as being continually in conversation with God. God whispers in our pleasures. The things we most enjoy—food, drink, sex, music, celebration—are intimations of his love. The trouble arises when we separate those pleasures from God's scheme and try to own and dominate them ourselves.

Another way God speaks to us is in our consciences. When we have violated God's rules, our consciences (if they are well formed) will torment us. We feel guilty, ashamed of our own wrongdoing. We want to be made clean and whole again. Some apologists say that conscience, the moral law written in our hearts, is one of our principal clues to the nature and presence of God. God leads us in the way of salvation if we are willing to listen for the instructions God gives.

And then there is the way God speaks in our pain. Maybe this is the trickiest communication of all. But scientists confirm that pain mostly functions to protect us. Pain alerts us that something is wrong and must be attended to. This notion that pain may work for our good is hard to accept. But often it is the best explanation we can find.

Recently a friend of mine was told by his doctor that he needed to check himself into the hospital for a heart catheterization. "The doctor may decide to do a balloon angioplasty or stents," our friend explained, "in which case I'll have to stay over." Within forty-eight hours we heard that he had undergone triple bypass surgery, a major intervention.

He was weak, worn out, and exhausted by his ordeal, but beginning to see the brighter side. "The good news is there's no damage to my heart," he explained. But what I kept noticing was how hard he had tried to postpone the treatment ("Couldn't it wait a few weeks?"). Maybe God was shouting, but my friend was ill disposed to hear.

I myself have behaved in this exact way, deaf to the smaller signals of trouble and able to listen only when the alarms were percussive and loud. Toughing it out, ignoring the worst—maybe sometimes these are good character traits. But sometimes they are only a kind of disobedience and pride. Several years ago I found myself on a gurney in the emergency room in Santa Fe, struggling with a severe rheumatoid arthritis attack. How had I ignored the warning signs? How had I gotten into such a mess? The rheumatologist, when he finally arrived, spent much of his time scolding me. "Are you aware what a serious illness you have?" "Have you been underreporting your symptoms to your doctor at home?" Apparently he thought I had not been listening to that persistent megaphone.

So in the school of adversity we are brought up short; we repent; we are changed. In spite of our rebellious hearts, we become submissive, obedient, grateful. The God who whispers, speaks, and shouts is always at our side and on our side. But faith is needed to admit our need for God. Faith is needed to listen and hear God's counsel. Faith is needed to believe that God wants the best for us, even when trouble strikes. As the psalm says, "A thousand may fall at your side, ten thousand at your right hand, but it will not come near you."

Tuesday of the Second Week

God wants our honest thoughts and feelings, as any lover does—not what we're supposed to say or feel.

—Murray Bodo

SOME FRIENDS OF MINE RECENTLY RETURNED from a visit to Italy, where they had seen the city of Pompeii, destroyed by a volcanic eruption in the first century after Christ. People who visit Pompeii often comment on the pornographic art displayed on the walls there. My friend, who was shocked as others have been, looked up at Mount Vesuvius and told God she understood why he had decided to wipe the place out.

"Oh, I hope that isn't true," I answered. "Because if it is, that means all the comments about God sending Katrina to destroy New Orleans might also be true." I have heard many discussions about God and hurricanes, about God and 9/11, God and the tsunami of December 2004. These are disasters of biblical proportions, and it is easy therefore to blame them on God.

Actually, I don't subscribe to the view that disasters are generally sent by God to chasten us. But as I reflected on this question, I realized I had never brought the matter up directly with God. That would be too awkward, too embarrassing! I'm the sort of person who shrinks from confronting God. I prefer to bury my questions under polite inquiries. I'm devious that way.

Now really, why would I do that? How can relationships be built on subterfuge? God wants our honest feelings. Abraham sets a fine example when he questions God about the people of Sodom. Would God spare the city if there were fifty good people there? Or forty? Or thirty? Or ten?

Elizabeth Kubler-Ross, an authority on death and dying, assures us that we can put our toughest questions to God. We can be angry with God. We can complain. The truth is, God can take it.

Even more important, God is seeking a genuine relationship. God wants more than a polite, diplomatic sort of conversation in which the cards are held close to the vest. He is looking for a frank and open dialogue. If we don't put our honest thoughts and feelings before God, we will never have a chance at a real exchange. In the spiritual life, such honesty is a fundamental, necessary surrender.

God says, "I don't want your sacrifices, your burnt offerings. What I want is you." Only our frankness will make such intimacy possible.

The truth is that we are often afraid to be open with God. We are not so fearful of unanswered prayers, though that is a serious issue. But what worries us more is what may happen if we make a real connection. Possibly God will ask something of us, expecting more than we are willing to give.

The Bible gives several examples of this kind of encounter:

When God asks Moses to help save the Israelites from Pharaoh, Moses does not want to accept the call. He challenges God's plan. And God challenges him. Their conversation is open, frank, plainspoken. "Who is in charge here?" is what God seems to say. Eventually, Moses has to back down.

In the New Testament, we see Jesus in dialogue with his Father. Sometimes that dialogue expresses simple trust: "I know, Father, that you always hear me." But sometimes Jesus seems to be holding back from following the Father's plan.

In the Garden of Gethsemane, Jesus asks his Father whether the "cup" can pass from him. He gets an answer, and he accepts it. But on the cross, he seems to be raising the question again. "My God, my God, why have you forsaken me?" This question is found in Psalm 22, so commentators may say that Jesus is only reciting Scripture in his prayer. All the same, the Scripture, spoken as a prayer from the cross, poses a challenge and question. Jesus is asking, openly and honestly, whether his Father has forsaken him.

In the Psalms we read this:

Sacrifice and offering you do not desire,
but you have given me an open ear.
Burnt offering and sin offering
    you have not required.
Then I said, "Here I am;
    in the scroll of the book it is
        written of me."

God welcomes our honesty. God is saying, "Show me the real person that you are."

Sometimes we are ashamed to be ourselves, before others and before God. Sometimes what we need most is to accept ourselves as we really are. Possibly we may need to change. In either case, as we see in Psalm 51, honesty is the place to begin: "The sacrifice acceptable to God is a broken spirit; a broken and contrite heart, O God, you will not despise."

This, too, is a small surrender, when we drop our masks and disguises and present ourselves authentically to God. It is another kind of repentance, a way to return.

Wednesday of the Second Week

Certain vocations, like that of raising children, offer a perfect setting for living a contemplative life. They provide a desert for reflection, a real monastery.

—Ronald Rolheiser

CERTAIN SPIRITUAL WRITERS LIKE TO MAKE this comparison: taking care of young children provides a desert for reflection, a real monastery. When they are your children, and you hear this pious observation, sometimes you want to throw up your hands. How in the world can young children leave us any time for reflection? They're always bombarding us with requests. *Can I have a drink of water? I want more juice! Can we go to the park? Can we watch a DVD? Let me play with blocks? Is it lunchtime yet? Can so-and-so come over to play?* Besides requests, there are objections and complaints. *I don't need to take a nap! No, I'm not hungry! I don't want to take a bath! It's not fair! He took my toys! She's mean! She messed up my puzzle! Are we there yet? We never get to do anything!* These are just a few samples of the constant barrage from children old enough to talk, to whine, to make their wishes known.

Yet I am sure the spiritual teachers who make this comparison are right. The best training ground for the spiritual life is not on smooth but rocky ground. When we want to grow in virtue, we do better in tough situations. It is easy to seem patient when nothing much is happening to challenge us. The real test of patience comes when any sane person would fly off the handle. Taking care of children is a perfect Los Alamos–style proving ground.

Years ago, when I first took up the spiritual life, I wanted to attempt some major penance. My spiritual director tried not to laugh. Finally, he said, "Better the penance you don't choose." His meaning was clear to me then. It is even clearer now. Life's tough situations can become a way to grow in stamina and virtue. The word "virtue" comes from the Latin for "strength." The monastery of child care is really our workout room, our gymnasium.

High-stress situations of all kinds—the office, the courtroom, the studio, the classroom—these are also schools of contemplation and virtue. But how? When in our imagination we briefly step outside of the situation, we see these circumstances as crucibles for prayer. When we stop to reflect on everyday challenges, we grasp what the real issues are.

Usually, we think of contemplation as taking place in solitude and silence. But many great spiritual teachers, Ignatius Loyola for one, say otherwise. They tell us to be contemplative in action. Contemplation is not entirely a function of where we are. No, contemplation is an inward disposition of the heart, intentionally quieting ourselves, turning to God whenever and wherever we can. To care for young children may prompt us to be glad for what has been given us. In the company of children we return to simplicity and discover our childlike hearts. When we care for young children, we learn attentiveness. Also, children remind us to laugh and play in ways that please God. Contemplation is about peacefulness, shalom. The monastery of childhood can encourage that peace in more ways than one.

One characteristic of children's lives is their regularity. The same is true of monasteries! Things happen in children's lives at predictable times:

mealtime, nap time, bath time, story time, out-door play. Dependable schedules give us hints of an inwardly peaceful universe, where order and harmony reign. Such pleasing regularity is also a clue to prayer. Today some of us are reviving the custom of fixed-hour prayer—the habit of prayer at certain times of day. That rhythm is consoling. Prayer is not just a duty to God but a reminder of God's abiding presence.

Jesus taught us about children and what we may learn from them. At his time in history, when children were often shunted aside, even underval-ued, Jesus brought children to center stage. "Let the little children come to me," he said, "and do not stop them, for it is to such as these that the kingdom of heaven belongs." Jesus also explains, "Whoever does not receive the kingdom of God as a little child will never enter it."

Imagine suggesting that we could learn from children! Jesus, as usual, challenged our precon-ceptions, our ways of being in charge. Jesus did not intend to give us a lecture on child care. Instead, he meant to encourage simplicity of heart.

Thursday of the Second Week

For a psychoanalyst to be any good . . . he'd have to believe that it was through the grace of God that he'd been inspired to study psychoanalysis in the first place.

—J.D. Salinger

TWO MODERN COMMENTATORS, WILLIAM A. Barry and William J. Connolly, both Jesuits, tell us of a common idea: the fear of consolation in prayer. As spiritual directors and teachers of spiritual direction they are informed by both Christian faith and psychotherapy. They want us to accept the life of grace through a rich, consoling, and comforting experience of prayer.

But sometimes we are afraid. We feel unworthy. We think we don't deserve this great onslaught of happiness. We resist. We are afraid to admit this resistance, even to ourselves! Modern spiritual direction, informed by psychological understanding, helps us to see the walls we may build against the joys of prayer. We are like people who think that medicines that taste bad are more efficacious. That is a psychological tic, one we may never fully eliminate, but which can be allowed for and understood.

In J.D. Salinger's book *Franny and Zooey,* a brother and sister spend time arguing about prayer. There is something both funny and insightful about the way they interweave insights from the Bible, Buddhist teachings, and *The Cloud of Unknowing* into a popular brew. Zooey is giving high-minded advice to his sister Franny about the Jesus Prayer: "Lord Jesus Christ, have mercy on me, a sinner." Zooey insists she should not use this prayer if she wants to get something out of it. Her motives must be purer than that. He is arguing for such detachment that only a highly advanced mystic should ever pray at all. Then Zooey finally winds up proclaiming, "Who in the Bible besides Jesus knew that we're carrying the Kingdom of Heaven around with us, inside where we're all too . . . stupid and sentimental and unimaginative to look?" And while Franny is still struggling to answer this, Zooey concludes by summing up the Jesus Prayer: "The Jesus Prayer has one aim and one aim only. To endow the person who says it with Christ-consciousness."

It's amazing to find all this religious thinking and sentiment folded into two long character sketches by J.D. Salinger.

We hardly expect Salinger to provide us insight into the path of surrender. But in these sketches what we find are some lessons about prayer, lessons in simplicity. The best way to approach prayer is the way Franny wants to: simply, and without overthinking it. The best way to resist a brother's (or anyone's) annoying interference in our prayer lives is not to let anyone or anything come between us and God.

Salinger's *Franny and Zooey* suggests that prayer is still a vital experience, needed by today's young people as much as in any past generation. The yearning to pray is human and fundamental. Prayer is the life's blood of our religion. It refreshes and sustains us.

Apparently, it is a natural human impulse to be afraid of good things, and to worry about our motives in desiring good things. But the best contemporary counseling says that prayer can and should be enjoyable. It should be our treasure. Where your treasure is, there shall your heart be also. As the psalm says, "in your right hand are pleasures forevermore."

Lord Jesus Christ, have mercy on me, a sinner. This is a lovely, biblical prayer that lends itself to gentle, consoling repetition. Prayer is an experience that has not been dislodged by contemporary psychology. In fact, psychology has helped us to understand how much prayer can delight and strengthen us. We need to enjoy prayer—that in itself may be a kind of surrender—and give way to the pleasures of being in the presence of God.

Are we alert to the mercies that fill our days?

—Kathy Coffey

ONE OF THE PRINCIPAL DISCIPLINES OF THE spiritual life is attentiveness: being alert to the simple, often subtle ways that God's grace enters our lives. Often, we have to set aside our anxious preoccupations in order to see that our days are filled with mercies. Or as one hymn puts it, "Morning by morning new mercies I see."

For several weeks now I have been watching an amaryllis plant grow. It is a potted plant, growing indoors from a bulb in an amphora-like pot. There are three of these plants near a window in the room where I write. The pots are made of some kind of plastic, but they look wonderfully like fired clay. On gray days, rainy days, cold days, cold nights, still this green shoot is springing up, and the buds are beginning to swell and bulge, reaching for the light. The green shoots seem to thicken, strengthen, turning into sheaths, with folded leaves pushing upwards. But these amaryllis flowers don't just burst into bloom; at least, not at first. For many days they seem to be on the verge of blooming, bright red petals poking free. Finally, the petals emerge, and there are not one, but four bright crimson flowers, four petals each. And that is only the first of three plants. Two more are beside it, struggling to blossom into life.

There is a small but lovely blessing in all this. The blessing comes not only when the flowers bloom, but when we *notice* them. To think we could have missed it! This exquisite beauty is right under our noses, but due to the stress and the demands of living, the phone calls, the deadlines, the schedules, the chores, the list-making—because of all these demands we could ignore the beauty within and inside of our daily routine.

Attentiveness is one way we appreciate God's mercies. But attentiveness is just a beginning. Beyond that is a level of reflection or interpretation. Beyond noticing these blooms, I can also compare these blooms to ourselves. First of all, their blooming begins in secret. And for the most part it continues in secret, hidden underground.

Not only that, the germination takes time. When we compare ourselves to the amaryllis buds working toward their destiny, we understand the virtue of patience. Weeks, not days, are needed for the amaryllis to bloom. All the more so for us.

And then, one day, the flowers come blazing forth. Their petals are delicate and frail, but they are shot through with bold, imaginative color. They proclaim a kind of victory. They have made a risky journey and have come at last into the light of day. The blooming process of the amaryllis—with all its inner struggle and effort and risk—reminds us of our own journeys. Our soul's journey takes place mostly in hiding, in secret, but at some point it breaks through in visible ways.

When I compare myself to the amaryllis, I see how inconstant I am. The amaryllis follows a path of simple obedience. But I am much more wayward. I am easily distracted, full of doubt, subject to discouragement, inclined to wander off track. Yes, I blame this on the human condition. But that's no excuse. When I can, I focus on the simple, straightforward nature of the spiritual path. Kierkegaard says, "Purity of heart is to will one thing." And Eugene Peterson has written a book with a title that speaks volumes about the spiritual life: *A Long Obedience in the Same Direction*.

For me, the amaryllis plant is a sort of herald. First it reminds me to be attentive, then to be an interpreter of grace. The amaryllis becomes for me a metaphor of obedience and surrender. This flower follows a track that comes from deep within, responding to something encoded in its nature. Lord, I ask, let me follow the simple amaryllis. May I go the way of small surrenders, so my soul may come fully into your glory.

Saturday of the Second Week

Sometimes there might be no words, but only a blank page created by silence and space. . . . But you are in the process of praying.

—Murray Bodo

I HAVE ALWAYS LOVED DR. PAUL TOURNIER'S story about his first attempt to pray with a pencil. He spent an entire hour with his journal open on the desk, his pencil poised in hand. At the end of the hour, nothing! He thought he had completely failed. But later he grasped the deep formation in that hour of wordlessness, the entering in, the letting go.

Where prayer is concerned, we are constantly entangled with "oughts." How ought we to pray? We imagine there is some approved, polished, sophisticated way to pray that we need to learn. When the disciples gathered around Jesus for instruction, they wanted him to give them the right words to say. He did so, and it's good to follow his approved text, the beautiful intentions we find in the Lord's Prayer.

But the blank page is also a grace. This page may be a literal blank sheet in a journal, lying open before us on the table. The page poses a question: What in the world do we want to say to God? We're tongue-tied, at a loss for words. Or the blank page may be figurative. There's no journal, no actual page, but what looms before us is emptiness. "I've drawn a blank," we sometimes say. We're stymied in our approach to God. We don't even know how to start the conversation.

Maybe it's a matter of taking turns. Maybe it's time for God to take the initiative, as the Lord has already done so many times. Maybe the blank page is our signal to rest and wait, to listen and receive.

Take it one step further. Possibly the blank page is a test, a trial, a kind of formation. Learning to be open and to wait may be entirely against the grain for us. We long to be filling up the journal with thoughts, ideas, requests. But God has something else in mind.

The blank page can be a way into solitude and silence, into contemplation, into prayer.

There are many deep theological words for this emptying of self. *Kenosis* is the term that scholars use for the self-emptying of Christ, who took the form of a slave. This kind of yielding, this surrender, is Christlike. We should allow this emptiness to form and shape us in the Lord's way. But so often we are thinking we must be in charge, we must take control. That is why the blank page is such a gift: it comes to us as a gift of grace, in the simplest, most ordinary way.

Even more, we must come to understand that this emptiness, this blank page, is prayer. It is more than an invitation to pray. It is actually prayer. We are making a small and needed surrender to the way things are: we are relenting, we are unwinding.

Those who truly pray understand this remarkable secret: the secret of emptying, and of the blank, unwritten page.

Third Sunday Through the Third Week of Lent

Pain and suffering are part and parcel of our planet, and Christians are not exempt.

—Philip Yancey

ONE OF THE MAIN QUESTIONS PEOPLE ASK me about prayer is why every prayer is not answered. That seems to fly in the face of what Jesus says and does. And this is one of the Lenten surrenders we can make. We can work to surrender our doubts about prayer.

Consistently, we associate Jesus with answered prayers. Jesus' teachings on prayer are straightforward and simple: "Ask and you shall receive; knock and it shall be opened to you." Jesus wants us to have a kind of sublime confidence. He often says that healings are more likely when people's faith is strong. Jesus makes us feel that God is always listening.

This confidence is especially keen before the raising of Lazarus. Jesus says, "Father, I thank you for having heard me. I knew that you always hear me, but I have said this for the sake of the crowd standing here, so that they may believe that you sent me." Lazarus has not yet been raised, but Jesus already knows that his prayer has been heard and answered. And Jesus wants us to know that the Father's generous response is not just for him, but also for us.

At the same time the Scriptures caution us against overconfidence in prayer. When Jesus struggles with Satan in the wilderness, Satan taunts Jesus into using prayer as a kind of magic bullet. He seems to want to distort Jesus' intimacy with God. "If your God is so terrific, and you're so close to him, why don't you just turn a few stones into bread? Why don't you jump off a high place and see if he'll save you? Why don't you come over to the dark side, where it's so much more fun?"

And Jesus replies that we should not test the Lord our God.

One of the deepest surrenders we are called to make (I'd hardly call it small) is when we must accept the death of someone we love.

Lieutenant Colonel Ken Brown, a chaplain with the United States Army 101st Airborne Division, serving in Iraq, has some insights on this theme. He wrote an entry in his war diary on April 9, 2003. He was commenting on soldiers who come face-to-face with death for the first time, when they see their comrades wounded or killed.

Some of these soldiers came to Chaplain Brown to talk about death.

"I had a young man come to me a couple of weeks ago . . . he talked to me about, if he had just been a couple of seconds sooner at a certain location, he could probably have prevented this or that." Soldiers feel guilty, Chaplain Brown says, because they didn't or couldn't prevent a buddy from dying. They feel guilty that they are still alive.

When soldiers actually see death, Brown says, their priorities change. He doesn't try to tell them that all this can be so easily explained. In the same way I think all of us feel a real anxiety about the things we can't seem to prevent through our prayer.

But Chaplain Brown tells his soldiers about a philosopher named Boethius, from the fourth century, who made a famous remark. When we come up against an evil, when God doesn't seem to be in charge, *God is writing straight with crooked lines.*

How do we reconcile this with the statement of Jesus, "I know, Father, that you always hear me"?

Jesus tells us to believe in a God of enormous power who surrounds us with his love. But sometimes it seems to us that this all-powerful God is not listening, is not responsive to our prayers. What then?

This experience—of sustained, unanswered prayer—is well known in the spiritual life. Sometimes it is called darkness. Sometimes it is called aridity, or dryness in prayer. It comes when we're not sure God is listening, when we think God doesn't care about us, when the outcomes we want are not forthcoming. This is a great test of faith.

The path leads both to the raising of Lazarus and to the Garden of Gethsemane. As Philip Yancey writes, "Pain and suffering are part and parcel of our planet, and Christians are not exempt." When we face this undesirable reality, when we accept that there will be pain and suffering in spite of our prayers, we accept God's wisdom as higher than our own. We trust that God is writing straight with crooked lines.

Even so, we continue to believe and to pray. We have faith that where our knowledge fails, God's knowledge does not.

This is an old map, one that has been folded and refolded many times, so creased it seems about to fall apart. Yet it leads us to hidden treasure, a deeper reliance on God. Where our treasure is, there will our hearts be also.

Monday of the Third Week

It is a good rule . . . to keep the clean sea breeze of the centuries blowing through our minds, and this can be done only by reading old books.

—C.S. Lewis

A PERSON WHO LIKES TO READ MAY FIND IT hard to think of reading during Lent as a small surrender. I am so inclined to reading that I forget to call it a spiritual practice. But reading spiritual books, especially older ones, can lead us to real spiritual depth. Our ancestors wrote and read spiritual books because this helped them to practice the spiritual life. This practice, which we call "spiritual formation" or "the spiritual life," seems rarer today. "The spiritual life" is not the latest buzzword.

To take the spiritual life seriously, I first had to learn what it was. Where did I find answers? In certain old books. There I discovered what C.S. Lewis calls "the clean sea breeze of the centuries blowing through our minds." I read *The Imitation of Christ* by Thomas à Kempis. I thumbed through *Introduction to the Devout Life* by Francis de Sales. I absorbed, not all at once, but slowly, *Abandonment to Divine Providence* by Jean-Pierre de Caussade. These books are centuries old, and are still in print.

I sampled some more recent books, too: *Practical Mysticism* and *The Spiritual Life* by Evelyn Underhill, and *Teach Us to Pray* by Andre Louf. Underhill (early twentieth century) was steeped in the spiritual writers of the past. Andre Louf is just seven years older than I. But since he is a very wise Cistercian monk, I thought he was centuries older.

Of course, it's not the oldness that makes these books so attractive. It is the wisdom. Spiritual classics ground us in age-old truth. They invite us to live the Christian life in a quietly authentic way. Most of these texts are short and are easy to slip into a briefcase for reading at odd moments throughout the day. These classics invite us to live in the presence of God wherever we are, whenever we can. So why not keep a book on hand that refreshes our knowledge of God, that leads us into devotion and prayer? Those are the clean sea breezes that Lewis talks about.

Sometimes spiritual classics may remind us about good ideas that are in danger of being forgotten. For instance, de Caussade writes about docility, a spiritual quality one rarely hears about. "If we are truly docile," he writes, "we shall ask no questions about the road along which God is taking us." De Caussade says we should give way to God and release our wills to be led in his way. "Divine action is always new and fresh, it never retraces its steps, but always finds new routes. . . . [T]hese paths are always opened in front of us and we are impelled along them." He is writing about the path of grace. "So what can we do except trust him?" He insists that God is our guide.

"Docility" is not a word we hear just every day. But it denotes a most desirable quality. "Docile" means "open to being led." You could say "docility" is another term for "small surrender." And we make such a small surrender when we take time for spiritual reading.

Recently I talked with a man who was excited about a modern book, *Addiction and Grace* by Gerald May. My friend was totally on fire about this book. It had provided him with new insights on his deepest questions. The writing was straightforward and to the point, telling illustrative and useful stories. It is not surprising that Gerald May, a modern author, is also steeped in the spiritual writing of the past. My friend found May's work a genuine spiritual discovery.

My simple conclusion is that the spiritual life flows deep, deeper than most of our everyday conversation. That is what we want and need, to move to a deeper level. Scripture leads us often to this deep place, to the depth and height and breadth mentioned in the letters of Paul. Some spiritual classics lead us there as well. Consider what Paul wrote to the Philippians so many centuries ago:

Finally, beloved, whatever is true, whatever is honorable, whatever is just, whatever is pure, whatever is pleasing, whatever is commendable, if there is any excellence and if there is anything worthy of praise, think about these things. Keep on doing the things that you have learned and received and

heard and seen in me, and the God of peace will
be with you.

In so many ways this ancient writing, when we
are surprised, even blindsided by it, comes to us
as a fresh sea breeze. Such writing reminds us to
plunge deep into the waters of grace.

Tuesday of the Third Week

There are many slow days when nothing seems to be happening. A lot of the Christian life develops underground when we aren't looking.

—Eugene H. Peterson

BECAUSE WE EXPECT, AND RIGHTLY SO, THAT Lent will be a time of transformation, we may be looking impatiently for signs of spiritual improvement. It's human, of course, to hold ourselves to a high standard. In fact, the life of spiritual formation used to be called "the life of perfection." It was guided by Jesus' command as given in the Gospel of Matthew: "Be perfect, therefore, as your heavenly father is perfect."

Today we have adjusted the language somewhat, in an effort not to be too driven. But our desire for God and godliness remains. Especially in Lent we take note of our failings. We resolve to do better about our imperfections. And we hanker for times of assurance, of consolation. We want to believe that we are getting somewhere. Lent, we think, should sharpen our edge in the moral life. And Lent, with its careful assignment of forty days, may heighten our expectations. We plan to accomplish something in Lent, to come closer to Jesus with seven-league boots. We look for the high drama of the spiritual life, the rewards, the destination.

Often this comes because we are so discontented with ourselves. We judge ourselves harshly and we feel that God is judging us the same way. In Jeremiah we read, "I the LORD test the mind and search the heart, to give to all according to their ways, according to the fruit of their doings." We look for external signs of our improvement. We are deeply impatient with our own imperfection.

That is why we should be glad of Eugene Peterson's comment: "There are many slow days when nothing seems to be happening." Another good insight is Peterson's sense that the Christian life develops underground. This is a fine agricultural metaphor. The seed of grace is planted deep within us. It is nurtured by time and our devotedness. If we are patient with ourselves, we will see the fruit of our Lenten diligence. But not all at once. Our goodness increases in fits and starts; it is nurtured underground. Partly we need to grasp that God is more patient than we are. God knows exactly who we are, what our dispositions are. What he wants from us is our hearts, not our burnt offerings. But we are harder on ourselves than God is. We make demands of God and of ourselves.

This struggle to appreciate God's boundless patience (and our own impatience) has been with us throughout the centuries. John Milton's life exemplifies this spiritual dilemma. Even as a young man, Milton dedicated himself to God and was impatient with himself for a lack of achievement. How, he asked himself, had he done so little by the age of twenty-three? How would God put up with his lack of accomplishment? He worried about a "late spring" that had shown no buds or blossoms.

But a much greater trial came at midlife, when Milton realized that he was going blind. He feared that loss of sight could ruin his life's dream of being a great Christian poet. Once again, Milton had to surrender his will and his expectations to the Almighty. Now, that is high drama! That is a huge scenario in the spiritual life. Milton's acceptance of the divine plan is a good example of surrender. Over and over in his life, he dealt with his worst temptations, pride, and impatience, and gave himself humbly to God. Perhaps that is why one of Milton's most quoted lines is this one: "They also serve who only stand and wait." Of course, he transcended his blindness by writing two epic poems and an amazing verse drama. But Milton is not a great spiritual example to us because he wrote great poems. He inspires us because he surrendered his life to God.

Our own surrenders may not be as dramatic as Milton's. Most of us don't have to deal with the onset of blindness in our forties. By and large, our lives are not scarred by great calamities. We have mood swings, all right. But they are modest, not titanic. Most of us, though we are ambitious, don't have the grandiose dreams of fame and glory that John Milton had.

Even so, we must practice submission and surrender, not once and for all, but over and over again. We must put aside our most outrageous dreams. We must set aside our false ideas of glamour and control. We must stand and wait. We must trust that the Christian life is growing within us in hidden ways.

This Christ-life is transforming us, but quietly. Gradually we begin to understand the long tradition of humility: not setting oneself up too high, or putting oneself down too low. And we must continue, we must persevere. We must apply ourselves to the spiritual disciplines. We must rejoice in the grace of God. We can't always notice the outward signs of our spiritual transformation. But we must trust in God's hidden wisdom. Everything is happening deep "underground."

Wednesday of the Third Week

Spiritual direction (means) entering into a friendship with another person in which an awareness and responsiveness to God's spirit in the everydayness of your life is cultivated. . . .

—Eugene H. Peterson

To pursue the spiritual life, should one have a spiritual director? For centuries, this worthy practice was principally connected to monasteries and religious houses, and more with high church than with low church. Some Roman Catholics and Anglicans might have spiritual directors. But Protestant Christians, equally devout, might not even have heard of such a thing.

In spiritual direction we surrender our daily lives to the work of the Holy Spirit by laying our lives before God and another person, in trust.

In one sense, spiritual direction is a form of witnessing to our faith. In church, when we are reciting professions of faith, we are of course saying what we believe. But when we set aside time to talk with a spiritual director about how God is working in our lives, we are first and foremost proclaiming that God *is* working. This is not only a profession of faith, it is a surrender. We open up to another person, and to God, our particular questions and dilemmas. Often, before the session begins, these questions loom very large. But once we have voiced the questions that weigh on our hearts, things come into proportion. Even before the director has a chance to comment, the Holy Spirit has apparently intervened, bringing a kind of peace and comfort into the situation.

Partly this is because of the level playing field laid out in the process. The director *takes on the role of confidant* and agrees to listen. The directee is also a confidant, one who agrees to open her soul in the conversation. But both persons open their souls, trustingly, before God. The director tries to help with interpretation, to give the other person perspective, often mentioning scriptural citations or Bible stories. Has the directee voiced a sense of inadequacy? Possibly the director might mention the story of Moses resisting God's call. Or maybe she will cite the experience of Samuel, who did not believe that God was speaking to him. The director tries not to tell her own stories unless they are directly on point. Even then the director should be sparing. She is there mostly to listen and interpret.

But both the participants in this process are together in order to listen to the Lord and to magnify the Lord. Spiritual direction can become a deeply valued aspect of our prayer lives. These relationships take on the character of friendships. In fact, they *are* friendships. But while the direction is in progress, it's good to keep these friendships dedicated for a purpose, different from the casual friendships we pursue in a more secular context. Although some directors work with groups, most of us think of spiritual direction as happening between two persons, one of whom is trained to listen for the work of the Spirit in another's life.

Sometimes, when preparing for a spiritual direction session, we think we have "nothing to say." *What in the world have I been doing since last time? Weren't there important issues? Didn't I have serious hangups?* We wonder how profitably—how spiritually—we have been using our time.

But as the session begins to unfold, we find that the ordinary business of living becomes a vast territory. The over-busyness of things, the weariness, the pressure, the passing of time, the particular burdens of an unexpected visitor, a major event that we find we are in charge of, the schedule, the expectations, the challenges of hospitality, the fretful interaction of the generations, the interplay of personalities—all these things and more provide the context of our lives. Shakespeare describes it well. Hamlet's words make perfect sense:

The slings and arrows of outrageous fortune. . . .
The insolence of office, and the spurns
That patient merit of the unworthy takes. . . .

Such are the ordinary challenges to our faith. Spiritual direction makes them bearable, lifts us above the fray. It is not that the director is all-knowing. Instead, the Holy Spirit breathes in and through the session, helping us to gain perspective on the daily trudge.

Jesus is our first teacher in the ancient art of spiritual friendship. In the Gospel of John he says: *You are my friends if you do what I command you. . . . I have called you friends, because I have made known to you everything that I have heard from my Father.* If we are cultivating responsiveness to and awareness of God's guidance in this friendship, we are on the right path.

Thursday of the Third Week

When you get a problem, present it to a counselor who knows what he's doing and doesn't hesitate to tell you. The Book of Proverbs suggests much the same.

—Thomas à Kempis

EVEN BEFORE I WAS A CATHOLIC, I HAD sense enough to take a serious moral problem to a trusted advisor. In my late teens and early twenties, when the problem was almost always men, I would find myself ringing the doorbell of the rectory and asking whether I could speak to someone. The odd thing was, I think I knew the answer already, but was blinded by my own willfulness.

The counselors who agreed to see me were not much older than I was; but they had been trained on how to deal with the pain, the embarrassment, the awkwardness. They put me at my ease. They showed me the right path. They helped me to feel that thousands had walked this path ahead of me. "You're not Catholic, so I can't give you absolution, but I'll give you a blessing."

In the New Testament I identified with the women who followed Jesus. Some were good women, like Mary of Bethany, who simply wanted to hear what Jesus had to say. Some were troubled women, like Mary Magdalene, from whom Jesus drove out seven devils. Some were unnamed, like the woman who came with perfume in an alabaster jar. The text in Luke says only that she was a sinner, and that Jesus treated her with compassion. He was criticized for his kindness. If Jesus were a real prophet, his critics said, he'd know better than to let himself be touched by a woman of the streets.

A similar story is told in the Gospel of John, with Mary of Bethany anointing the feet of Jesus. In this case, Mary's perceived transgression is in wasting the costly perfume. Jesus forgives and defends her.

Then there is the woman taken in adultery. By a clever approach, Jesus prevents her from being stoned: "Let anyone among you who is without sin be the first to throw a stone at her." He is compassionate. "Has no one condemned you?" "No, sir." "Neither do I condemn you." He tells her to go and sin no more.

Through the centuries, people have brought their problems to Jesus Christ—in sacramental ways and ways that are more informal. He has ministers on earth who can listen compassionately as he did, and give the kind of wise advice that he would give. Lent is a good time to open our hearts about a spiritual problem, to unburden our souls. Often, when we have done so, we feel a lighter step, a renewed sense of freedom.

Thomas à Kempis tells us to find a wise counselor for advice when any problem arises. Jesus is the wisest of counselors, and has empowered many to speak and forgive in his name.

Don't think about being good! If you accept the very tiresome stuff the Lord is handing out to you, that's all he wants at the moment.

—Evelyn Underhill

O NE GREAT PITFALL OF THE SPIRITUAL LIFE is self-preoccupation. When we attempt to live virtuously and decide to turn inward for God's sake, we may accidentally miss the target and spend too much time thinking about ourselves. In this self-conscious mode, we can become morose, depressed, or discouraged. Or else we can swing in the opposite direction and find we're on cloud nine, maybe a little too inclined to congratulate ourselves for how well we're doing in the spiritual life. Evelyn Underhill is one of the best guides on how to avoid these complications.

What makes Underhill a wise guide to simplicity? This twentieth-century Anglican writer was thoroughly immersed in ordinary life. Although she studied the great mystics and wrote about mystical experience, her approach to living was down-to-earth and practical. (Her modest but persuasive book *Practical Mysticism* offers a clue to her straightforward approach.)

A married woman from the middle class who never earned a theological degree, Underhill learned the spiritual life not only by her reading, but by friendship with some great Christian teachers. Baron Friedrich Von Hugel, an important Roman Catholic scholar, served as Underhill's spiritual director, friend, and mentor.

In her writing, Underhill stays focused on surrender and simplicity. She knows about the Christian joys, the upper reaches of the mystical life, but she advises us never to strive for such things. Instead, she reminds us that the great mystics were simple, easygoing, peaceful, often lighthearted.

Underhill knows that those who practice the spiritual life may be hard on themselves. She knows that they are subject to bouts of religious romanticism. To burst that balloon, she reminds us of the grace found in ordinary living. "Consider the sequence of daily acts, and your external interest as part of your service, part of God's order for you, and as having a proper claim on your undivided attention."

The more we are serious about Lent, the more we need to learn simplicity. The Lenten journey seems long and demanding. And we're tempted to magnify the effort of our Lenten practice, to assign ourselves a high and prestigious role as spiritual mountain climbers. We focus on ourselves instead of contemplating the Lord.

To live spiritually, however, is to live unselfconsciously, without putting on airs or condescending to others. Underhill cautions against "struggle" and against another pitfall she calls "vehemence." To show the disadvantage of trying too hard, she describes trying to quiet a baby or a pet with "struggle" and "vehemence." Instead, we should radiate a peaceful spirit, practice detachment, and become like little children.

To one of her correspondents, Evelyn Underhill writes, "Drop religion and just be quiet and wait a bit. . . ." Does she really mean for us to drop religion? I think she means exaggerated religious preoccupation, which is a pain to oneself and others at any time. She sees that a constant struggle to live spiritually can become a drive for success rather than reliance on God's grace.

The idea is to forget yourself and remember God. "Just plain self-forgetfulness is the greatest of graces. The true relation between the soul and God is the perfectly simple one of childlike dependence." In the history of Christian practice, how much ink has been spilled to convince us of this? Yet, because of our complex personalities, we have to learn this simple truth over and over again.

Saturday of the Third Week

*Blessed are those who trust in the L*ORD,
*   whose trust is the L*ORD.
They shall be like a tree planted by water,
*   sending out its roots by the stream.*

—Jeremiah

ONE OF THE THINGS WE WANT IN LENT IS TO grow in virtue. But how does that happen? Often we may do so through our friendships. When we choose our friends, we are choosing the good qualities they exemplify. We may not do this consciously, but one of our hidden motives in friendship is to find people who inspire us, who make life richer or more valuable.

C.S. Lewis describes the good influence of friends in his autobiography, *Surprised by Joy*. In his mid-twenties Lewis had returned to his studies at Oxford after serving in the First World War. He went into a discussion class in English literature with about ten or twelve students. And there he made a new friend, Nevill Coghill. The minute Coghill started speaking, Lewis knew he was clearly different from the other people who were there; and Lewis thought right away that this was a man after his own heart.

Lewis was surprised to make a new friend so suddenly. He thought maybe he had outgrown the instantaneous friendships of his younger days. But soon he realized that Coghill wasn't just the smartest one in the class, but he was also a Christian and a sincere believer. Some other things about this young man struck Lewis as being attractive and unusual—old-fashioned things. Nevill Coghill was a kind of a throwback to another era. In him Lewis observed chivalry, honor, courtesy, "freedom," and "gentilesse."

Lewis had another friend named Owen Barfield, who was also beginning to overthrow his ideas about the modern world. Lewis was beginning to suspect that the modern world was not really so great after all. People like Barfield and Coghill were practicing the virtues of the past, and they were changing the way that C.S. Lewis thought and felt about just about everything.

Lewis was laboring under the belief that virtue had somehow gone out of date. He was in the grip of chronological snobbery, the view that modern ideas are better than ancient or medieval ones. But these two friends, who thought otherwise, convinced him that virtue is timeless and can be lived today as effectively as in any other era.

When we ourselves are feeling a lack in modern life; when we think that our leaders are slippery; when we think that our athletic heroes are troubled; when we worry that the film stars and film writers who ought to be the sources of enlightenment for us are instead developing their values out of a culture of addiction, rather than a culture of grace—that's when we need the virtuous life: acquired virtues of prudence, justice, temperance, and fortitude. They are acquired, because the more you practice them the more they increase. Undergirding these, and strengthening them, are the infused virtues of faith, hope, and charity.

Are these the virtues of an earlier time? Were earlier centuries really so wonderful? There is reason to suppose the Middle Ages were a terrible time, a time of wicked courtiers, acquisitive dictators, feudal enslavement, all the sins that flesh is heir to. But the Lord does not forsake us in any time; in any generation virtues are possible through grace.

The prophet Jeremiah says that when our hearts turn away from the Lord, we become like scrub trees in the desert. We live in a parched and desolate land. We hardly even notice when relief is on the way! But Jeremiah shows us another view of the one who trusts in God. This person is

... like a tree planted by water,
    sending out its roots by the stream.
It shall not fear when heat comes,
    and its leaves shall stay green.

How can we become trees that bloom in the desert? One way to practice this hardy, virtuous life is to gather with a group of friends to study, more deeply, the life of the Spirit. Bible studies may offer this. Groups that form to pursue any common interest—history, the arts, literature— may offer a strengthening of virtue.

Good friends are a blessing. God sends them, I think, to shape us in the life of faith. Friendship is still another way we may open ourselves up to the life of grace.

Fourth Sunday Through the Fourth Week of Lent

Fourth Sunday in Lent: Laetare Sunday

Monday of the Fourth Week

Tuesday of the Fourth Week

Wednesday of the Fourth Week

Thursday of the Fourth Week

Friday of the Fourth Week

Saturday of the Fourth Week

Fourth Sunday in Lent: Laetare Sunday

Our religion is not pure detachment or pure attachment.
It's a dance between the two.

—Richard Rohr

TODAY, THE FOURTH SUNDAY OF LENT, IS known as "Laetare Sunday." *Laetare* is the Latin word meaning "to be happy." At church, the celebrant wears a rose vestment instead of the customary purple of the Lenten season. Purple is the defining penitential color of the season. But rose is a lovely interruption, a color of rejoicing to remind us that Easter is not far off. This is a good day to entertain friends, or to go to the circus!

Such intertwining of death and life, sorrow and rejoicing, is always part of the Christian message. Ours is a religion of heartbreak and of celebration, a message of God's deep love for his wounded world. Richard Rohr says that our religion helps us to dance between attachment and detachment, gain and loss.

I'm always surprised when dancing is used as a religious or a spiritual metaphor. Perhaps that is because I think of religion and the sacred as something high and serious. Oh yes, I know that King David danced before the ark, but wasn't that a dangerous thing to do? Doubtless the example of Shaker dancing should reassure me. *'Tis a gift to be simple, 'tis a gift to be free, 'tis a gift to come round where we ought to be.* . . . The Shakers were spare, lean, self-denying folks, but still they danced to express their religious joy. Especially in Lent, we're inclined to become Puritans, dressing ourselves and our dispositions in varying shades of beige and gray.

Richard Rohr employs this dancing metaphor advisedly. He is one of our best teachers of both contemplation and action. His insights are deeply incarnational, and he shows us how to be both attached and detached in an inspired kind of balance. He knows that such contrasted disciplines are two blades of a scissors, effective when they work together. Rohr constantly relies on curious comparisons to show us the central mysteries of spiritual life. For example, he says that our spirituality grows not by addition but by subtraction. As we become simpler, as we own less and traffic with fewer things, our hearts are lighter, our joy is greater. We shed our burdens. We're ready to step lightly, to trip the light fantastic. Christianity allows us to dance between detachment and attachment—between owning and giving away, between caring for our own and caring for those we do not know. It's a rhythm of life that is neither too worldly nor too ascetical.

One of the loveliest ideas in Judaism is the repair of the world: *tikkun olan*. For a long time I was deeply moved by this idea but did not fully understand it. I imagined that the repair of the world was something God wanted from us, like love of neighbor and social responsibility. I was wrong. The repair of the world—*tikkun olan*—is something that God is doing. His almighty power is mending our brokenness. To facilitate this, what we need to do is pray to God and be obedient to his commands.

The church fathers used an even more startling expression. They described the Trinity as a Great Round Dance, in which love and power are constantly flowing from One to Another. This divine communication, a deep melody, continues night and day. It is a harmony, timeless and eternal, the music that upholds creation, outside of us but constantly bathing us in sound.

Laetare Sunday makes its rosy appearance in the middle of Lent to remind us of the happy ending to our story and to the Christ story. The Father in Heaven has sent us his Son because he so loved the world, and us. As we walk through the days of Lent, we retrace a path of obedience leading to both sorrow and joy, to the ultimate *Gloria*. Thomas Merton tells us that "no despair of ours can alter the reality of things, or stain the joy of the cosmic dance which is always there.... We are invited to forget ourselves on purpose, cast our awful solemnity to the winds and join in the general dance."

Monday of the Fourth Week

The whole house seemed soaked in love and prayer. . . . (The place) cured solitude and gave me at last really the feeling of belonging to the Christian family. I lost here my last bit of separateness and wish for anything of my own and gained a wholly new sense of the realness and almost unbearable beauty of Christian life.

—Evelyn Underhill describing
her retreat at Pleshey

RETREAT HOUSES ARE OFTEN BEAUTIFUL, not in the worldly way of having fine furnishings and possessions, but in the unworldly way of bringing us into the presence of God. We may find ourselves in a country setting, where windows or balconies take us near a river or give us a mountain view. There may be flowers in bloom. One fine retreat house in Texas has many short texts of poetry and Scripture displayed on stones. These are striking; they speak to us when we pray.

But I have also learned this about retreat houses: they are places of hospitality, all right, but we must come to them with an open heart, an interior disposition to grace. It is our open-heartedness that makes the place beautiful. We have gone there in hopes of a meeting with Jesus Christ, Our Lord. That inner disposition is what counts.

To make a retreat, even of a few hours, in Lent, is a small surrender. By doing so—not necessarily in a retreat house, but in any place of quietness and refuge—we open our souls to God's grace.

"Welcome to the desert," said Father Dave Denny on my first visit to Nada Hermitage near Crestone, Colorado. I had heard about the place and had always wanted to make a silent retreat in a hermitage. Always romantic about the spiritual life, I thought a few days as a hermit would suit me fine.

I kept silence with few exceptions for a week. There were stretches of beautiful, intense solitude. Only two meals were prepared for the retreatants. The rest we prepared on our own, using little stoves in our small hermitage houses. In the garden, I pulled up fresh vegetables: eggplant, cucumbers, carrots. We were open to the beauty of the outdoors. Through the window of my hermitage at dawn, I saw deer—just shadowy outlines—moving past. One night I went down to the chapel for an hour of Eucharistic adoration; I left the hermitage at close to 4:00 AM, and walked, snuffing my electric torch, under a night sky blazing with stars. I was moved by the monastic style of the place, with young postulants going barefoot into the chapel, wearing rough brown monkish garments complete with hoods. A bit of Latin came back to me: *Cucullus non facit monacum:* "the hood doesn't make the monk." A little twelfth-century humor goes down well at a desert hermitage.

Modern life was not completely absent. I had brought a laptop with me, but the sunlight streaming through my windows made it hard to read the screen. Not far from me was an office with a computer and Internet service. There, I heard the unmistakable hum of a Xerox machine. If I made arrangements, I could make a long-distance call. I was conscious that those who lived there year-round had plenty of cares and concerns. Running a retreat house kept their lives busy, like the busy life we had left behind. We who had come to bask in their hospitality were temporarily set free.

Each small hermitage had a name. This, too, was a way we could respond to grace. I opened my heart to saints like Teresa of Avila and John of the Cross when I saw the hermitages named for them. I opened my heart to Jesus most of all. In the library I found countless books, recordings of talks by great retreat masters, and solitude. The modern building had been designed by a contemporary architect to evoke a long monastic tradition. The chapel was modest, but lovely. Everywhere I found sweet places to reflect and pray.

Nada Hermitage followed a modified monastic rule in the Carmelite tradition. The members of the community told me about Elijah at Mount Carmel, tracing their biblical origins. They kept the grand silence. At noon they rang the Angelus, and prayed. On certain nights they kept a vigil. It was all prayerful, peaceful, and evocative.

As I walked along the stony path, I remembered the words of Psalm 91:

For he will command his angels concerning you . . .
so that you will not dash your foot against a
stone.

At some distance down the road, there were
stations of the cross. They were tall and spare, an
invitation to walk the sorrowful path with Jesus.

Whether a retreat house is old or new, whatever
tradition it keeps, whether the food is generous or
sparse, whether the desert is real desert with sand,
or is a desert in the midst of the city, there is a
blessing in a Lenten retreat lasting one day, three
days, or more.

We are following the custom of Jesus, who
went apart to pray. And when we do this, we find
him there.

Tuesday of the Fourth Week

We need a theology that teaches us that even though we cannot unscramble an egg God's grace lets us live happily and with renewed innocence. . . . [T]ime and grace wash clean.

—Ronald Rolheiser

THIS SEASON OF REPENTANCE CALLS US TO another kind of surrender: reconciliation. We search our hearts in hopes of forgiveness, not only wanting God to forgive us but also to forgive ourselves. Some of us carry the early memory of our own wrongdoing long after God and others have forgiven us. Not realizing it, we hold onto our regrets. We forget that time and grace wash clean.

Jesus teaches us about God's forgiveness. But sometimes we are reluctant to believe in such a compassionate and forgiving God. If we have done something to hurt a marriage, a friendship, a family relationship, we refuse to let it go. Do we believe, fully, that repentance can restore us? That we can be reconciled?

Lent is a good time to reassess our understanding of God. If a parent or teacher has formed our idea of God as a hard taskmaster, we may need to revise our theology. Often a new sense of forgiveness begins when we admit these inward feelings about God. Anger against God can be buried very deep.

People sometimes can't forgive what they think God has done wrong. A friend of mine once told me she could not forgive God because of the Holocaust. It was easier for her to become an atheist than to work out what kind of God would permit such evil. In a similar statement for National Public Radio, the comedian Penn Jillette said: "Believing there is no God means the suffering I've seen in my family, and indeed all the suffering in the world, isn't caused by an omniscient, omnipresent, omnipotent force. . . . ." In the same essay series, Bill Nunan, a scientist, describes how he has revised his conception of God to fit with his knowledge of science. I don't accept Nunan's theology. But I do understand what is driving him. He does not want to retreat into atheism. So he has refocused his picture of God.

Sometimes people recovering from pain say they have rejected religion in favor of spirituality. Alas, every spirituality hangs on a theology, even when that theology is unspoken. The best theological starting point in Scripture is in the First Letter of John: "God is love." John's letter continues: "And those who abide in love abide in God, and God abides in them." If we begin with a childlike spirit and a loving God, we will soon arrive at the kind of religion taught by Jesus. Jesus maintains high moral principles but allows for human weakness. That is the Jesus whom Father Rolheiser wants us to understand.

Rolheiser speaks of being raised in a church with an unsparing moral code. "I was raised in a Catholicism which was deeply moral. It took commitment seriously and called sin sin. It was, on most moral issues, brutally uncompromising." Looking back, Rolheiser values the clarity of that upbringing, contrasted with the moral relativism of today. But he thinks that worldview was sometimes unforgiving and lacking in compassion, in giving second chances. "We need a theology that teaches us that even though we cannot unscramble an egg God's grace lets us live happily and with renewed innocence. . . ." He calls this a theology of brokenness, adding that we must learn that "time and grace wash clean."

Recently I shocked a room full of women by telling them the story of Dorothy L. Sayers and the child she had out of wedlock. The year was 1923, the pregnancy was unplanned, Sayers was not married, and the father refused to take responsibility for the child. Sayers took a leave from her job in London, gave birth to her baby in a discreet country hospital, and placed the boy with her aunt and cousin, who cared for him. Later, when Sayers married, she intended to claim the child as her own, but did not. When the boy was about ten, "Cousin Dorothy" and her husband said they would adopt him. In fact, no adoption was legally necessary and none took place. For years she provided his financial support and paid for his Oxford education. But the young man did not know Dorothy L. Sayers was his mother until after her death. This incident shows what can happen in harshly judgmental societies when reconciliation is lacking.

In today's more tolerant atmosphere, it is hard to understand why an enlightened woman would engage in such deception, risking her own emotions and her son's self-esteem to protect them both from social stigma. To me, the story has a special power. It underscores the bitterness of a world without Christian forgiveness. It shows how much we need time and grace to wash us clean. Dorothy L. Sayers paid for her son's upbringing and education. But, hemmed in by social stigma, she never went far enough to be reconciled to him.

Is there a value in such a painful memory? Perhaps it is only this, that in our own lives we may need to surrender our pride and break barriers to forgive and to be reconciled. This Lent, may we surrender not only our sins, but the memory of our sins, to the grace that washes clean.

*So, when you are offering your gift at the altar, if you
remember that your brother or sister has something against
you, leave your gift there before the altar and go; first be
reconciled to your brother or sister, and then come and offer
your gift.*

—Matthew

SOMETIMES WE HAVE PROMPTINGS THAT
remind us of unfinished business. We know
in our hearts that a surrender is required, though
perhaps we do not feel equal to it.

For years, I felt a pang whenever I heard the
text from Matthew about being reconciled to your
brother or sister. But I did not know how to effect
a reconciliation with my half-brother Charles, the
only child of my father's second marriage. I had
not seen him since he was about six or seven years
of age. I was in college then, in New Orleans. My
father used to drive from Lake Charles, Louisiana,
where he lived with his second family, to visit me.
And he would bring Charlie along.

Charlie was a charming and attractive child, but somehow I never came to think of him as my brother. In those days divorce was still considered very shameful. The easygoing customs that now prevail, with divorced parents taking turns in caring for their children, had not yet taken hold. I saw Charlie when he was a small child. Then I moved to New York City and completely lost track of him. My father died, and it seemed he was the only link that Charlie and I might have had.

What had kept us apart? Was I resentful that my father had left my mother and me for a second family? No doubt. But there was another obstacle: our mothers, who had kept us firmly separated during their lifetimes.

About ten years ago, when both mothers had died, Charlie and I had a kind of reconciliation. It came about through a cousin, who wanted to see us get together again. Charlie and his wife, my husband and I, and cousin Joan got together for lunch at a New Orleans restaurant. I was eager, but apprehensive, in having this long-standing matter finally settled. The restaurant was not

crowded that day. I remember we laughed with
the *maitre d'* about our "long-lost brother and
sister" reunion, joking that it was like those rec-
onciliations you see on television shows.

I was relieved to find that we liked Charlie and
his wife, and that Charlie did not have a striking resemblance to my father. He must look more
like his mother, I found myself thinking. I felt a
kind of sorrow at the long years when we had not
known each other. But I also felt a genuine sense
of gratitude that those years were over.

Since that time, we have exchanged Christmas
cards and invitations to major events in our
lives. But it will never be possible to mend this
relationship fully. The years when Charlie and I
might have known each other as brother and sister are gone. Possibly it would never have felt like
a relationship of siblings; after all, there are fifteen
years of difference in our ages.

But peacemaking is a very good thing. I know
how hard, how painful, how awkward it was to
effect just this one small reconciliation when no
great issues were at stake. Our father had died
long before. Now Charlie's mother and mine had

also died. There was nothing "standing in our way" except the memory of past sorrow. I haven't felt any great waves of consolation about this. Possibly I will never fully unpack the meaning of divorce upon my life and Charlie's. But I do have a sense of relief.

> You have heard that it was said, "An eye for an eye and a tooth for a tooth." But I say to you . . . if anyone strikes you on the right cheek, turn the other also; and if anyone wants to sue you and take your coat, give your cloak as well; and if anyone forces you to go one mile, go also the second mile. Give to everyone who begs from you, and do not refuse anyone who wants to borrow from you.

The reconciliation we look for in Lent is not only with God but with others. The Gospel says clearly that, if we want a relationship with God, we should make peace with each other. To be a Christian is to mend a quarrel. Are there issues in our lives, below the surface, in need of God's healing grace? Sometimes this peacemaking is not entirely our own doing. It comes when Jesus speaks in our hearts, and we try to imitate him; it comes when we cooperate. There is a real surrender in obedience to God's word.

Thursday of the Fourth Week

She held up her hand and then knocked it several times against the wall. "This is just a wall. Someday it will disintegrate. Someday this house will be gone, even without a storm. All that we lost was material things. We survived."

—Katrina survivor on the
Mississippi Gulf Coast

ONE OF THE SURRENDERS WE MAKE DURING Lent is to practice mercy. We are following Jesus' teaching, "Blessed are the merciful, for they will receive mercy."

In Matthew's Gospel, Jesus develops this teaching further. The Son of Man is represented as a king who comes to judge the world in the end time: "Then he will say to those at his left hand, 'You that are accursed, depart from me . . . for I was hungry and you gave me no food, I was thirsty and you gave me nothing to drink, I was a stranger and you did not welcome me, naked and you did not give me clothing, sick and in prison and you did not visit me.'" The listeners respond in confusion. "Lord, when was it that we . . . did not take care of you?" The king continues, "Just as you did not do it to one of the least of these, you did not do it to me."

Often we find this teaching overwhelms us. The reach of global poverty and need, the depth of need in our own communities, is huge. Where do we begin?

We respond to this teaching of Jesus in simple ways. To surrender an afternoon as a hospital volunteer is a work of mercy and kindness. To get out a hammer and nails on a Saturday morning to finish a Habitat for Humanity house is also a small surrender.

And sometimes the chance to do a spiritual work of mercy comes out of nowhere, as it did to me when I was invited to lead a day of prayer for Gulf Coast residents still dealing with Hurricane Katrina. This spiritual work of mercy—to comfort the afflicted—requires a certain tact and sensitivity. A year and a half after a major disaster, these survivors were still hurting. How could I comfort them? Words of Jesus came to mind. "Do not store up for yourselves treasures on earth, where moth and rust consume and where thieves break through and steal; but store up for yourselves treasures in heaven, where neither moth nor rust consumes and where thieves do not break in and steal. For where your treasure is, there will your heart be also."

But would these be the right thoughts to bring to Katrina survivors? Does one comfort the afflicted by saying the personal possessions they have lost are not so important after all?

In the middle of all my pondering, a letter came from a friend who knew about my speaking invitation. She had gathered several Gulf Coast "survival stories" from those whose faith had guided them. One person had said, "When your friend, Ms. Griffin, comes to encourage people, ask her to be encouraged by those who survived. They used remarkable survival skills as they leaned on their faith in God to see them through."

One story was about two women friends who swam to safety when the waters rose, even though one of them had only partly recovered from a hip replacement. Clinging to a boat, they waited five or six hours for rescue. Another story concerned a woman whose leg was gouged by a desk floating by in her flooded living room. Several days later a doctor recognized her wound as life-threatening. This woman told how she called on her faith to brave the pain and the surgeries.

Still a third survivor's home had been reduced to a concrete slab. She said about her loss: "Sometimes I think of the things that meant something to me . . . things that people had given me. I remember letters I had saved and all the family photographs. Yet I know these are all just things."

These survivors insisted that God had been with them and beside them, protecting them. They didn't blame God for their injuries; they didn't blame God for the storm. Instead, they blessed him for their recovery.

Through this kind of mutuality I was able to practice mercy, by bringing Jesus again to Katrina survivors who were already living by faith. I went to comfort them; but they also comforted me. I shared with them what they already knew: what Jesus says about founding our house upon the power and grace of God. "Everyone then who hears these words of mine and acts on them will be like a wise man who built his house on rock. The rain fell, the floods came, and the winds blew and beat on that house, but it did not fall, because it had been founded on rock."

To offer Christ's mercy is to receive Christ's mercy. This surrender brings its own beatitude. However inadequate we may feel to practice a spiritual work of mercy, we should do it sensitively. It is good work, in Lent or any other time. It is the Lord's work on earth.

The hair shirt, worn by Sir Thomas More for many years and sent to Margaret Roper the day before his martyrdom, is preserved by the Augustinian canonesses of Abbots Leigh, Devonshire, to whom it was brought by Margaret Clements, the adopted child of Sir Thomas.

—The Catholic Encyclopedia

THOMAS MORE, AT ONE POINT IN HIS LIFE, considered entering a monastery. Instead he remained a layman, becoming a husband and father. He was prominent in the law and later a minister in Henry VIII's government. Yet he never gave up a serious practice of the spiritual life. Though he was vigorously employed, he set aside one day a week for solitude and prayer. And among other severe spiritual practices he wore a hair shirt.

A hair shirt is a penitential garment worn next to the skin for the specific purpose of making the wearer uncomfortable. In some ways it is akin to the sackcloth we read of in the Bible—a rough kind of cloth, maybe something like today's burlap, that was worn at times of mourning or grief. But sackcloth was worn to be seen, as a public sign of one's sorrow. The hair shirt was worn in secret. And the main point of wearing such an uncomfortable garment was to keep the body in check.

In earlier times, many severe forms of penitence were practiced. Modern people, Catholics included, may consider these practices extreme. Today, the Catholic Church, when encouraging Lenten discipline, wants us to know what Jesus said about it, and to remind us of the inner meaning of whatever practices we may take on. Jesus himself was concerned about holy practices becoming superficial, being done without a sincere intention of the heart. In Matthew's Gospel we find him saying, "Whenever you pray, do not be like the hypocrites." "Whenever you fast, do not look dismal." "When you give alms, do not let your left hand know what your right hand is doing." Secrecy, privacy are important. But not in and of themselves. Jesus wants us to pray, fast, and give alms with sincerity. And he does not want us to engage in these practices for show.

That is the standard by which our own Lenten fasting and discipline should be reviewed and considered. Yes, it is fun to tell all our friends and neighbors what we are giving up for Lent. But definitely, when we do that, we have let both the left hand and the right hand know what we are doing. It is much better, if we're able, to take on some form of self-denial quietly, without mentioning that we have given it up for Lent. Of course, if people press you about why you're not taking a drink, it may be wise to give a reason, if only to relieve the pressure. But in fact, you're not obligated to explain.

Always, Jesus says, the outward practice should reflect an inward disposition of the heart.

Penitence should first of all be understood very broadly: apologizing to an injured party or making amends, healing family divisions, cheerfully taking on menial tasks. Among these practices, fasting is probably the one most often encouraged, during Lent or any time. Penitence—whether fasting or some other kind of constraint—should open us up daily to the Holy Spirit. A passage in Isaiah reveals what God desires from us when we fast:

Is not this the fast that I choose:

> to loose the bonds of injustice,

> to undo the thongs of the yoke,

to let the oppressed go free,

> and to break every yoke?

Is it not to share your bread with the hungry,

> and bring the homeless poor into your house;

when you see the naked, to cover them,

> and not to hide yourself from your own kin?

Perhaps the most overlooked form of penitence comes during our celebration of the Eucharist. We're so used to it, we almost forget it is there: there is an hour's fast before receiving Holy Communion, and this we observe whenever we attend Mass. But just as important, during Mass, we make a general confession of our sins. In earlier days, some would strike their breasts as an expression of penitential sorrow. Though this gesture is no longer seen often, it may be used devotionally by some.

When did Thomas More wear his hair shirt? Not only in the Lenten season, but also throughout the year. Apparently, he needed a physical reminder of his mortality. Also the shirt, rubbing against his skin, reminded him of the sufferings of the Lord.

For him, this was a small surrender, calling to his mind the Lord who had suffered for his sake. We, too, are looking for reminders of the Lord, ways to unite ourselves with the sacrificial love and suffering of Christ. Our modest penitential practices in Lent—things we give up, things we do without, things we do on purpose in charity— all these are reminders of Jesus' love for us, and the sacrifice he made for our salvation. They help us to walk with Jesus to Calvary and beyond.

But now what do I do? How do I give up control? Please, Jesus, teach me your way of relinquishment.

—Richard J. Foster

In Matthew's Gospel, Jesus says, "Blessed are the meek, for they will inherit the earth." This is a hard teaching when we hear it said or see it written. Our whole cultural formation is toward winning, being in charge. We are afraid of weakness. Words like "meekness" and "surrender" sounds like defeat.

But the Christian life, in some mysterious way, turns everything inside out. Why is this Christian reversal a good idea? Jesus repeatedly tells and shows us why these seemingly paradoxical teachings are good and true. God the Father has a greater design, a better plan than we could devise for ourselves.

During an interview about his acceptance of Christian faith, C.S. Lewis was asked about how he experienced the turning point of his conversion.

He said: "I seemed to hear God saying, 'Put down your gun and we'll talk.'" The comparison was drawn from Western movies. It was typical of Lewis's sense of humor.

In a more elaborate account of his own conversion, Lewis described surrender another way. He spoke of God having "closed in" on him while he was riding up Headington Hill, near Oxford, on the top of a double-decker bus. It is striking how Lewis remembered not just the interior movement of the spirit but also the actual locale. Slowly, something about himself began to become clear. "I became aware that I was holding something at bay, or shutting something out. Or, if you like, that I was wearing some stiff clothing, like corsets, or even a suit of armor, as if I were a lobster. . . ."

Later in the same passage he made another comparison. He said he felt like a man of snow at long last beginning to melt. "The melting was starting in my back drip-drip and presently trickle-trickle. I rather disliked the feeling."

What Lewis described was, first, his resistance (the lobster shell, the suit of armor, the coating of snow) and then how he let his defenses down. In a rather striking parallel to this homely personal account, Lewis uses a similar snow metaphor in his children's stories, to describe the imaginary kingdom of Narnia. An evil witch has cast a spell on the place, and it is always winter. But when the messianic lion Aslan comes, the snow begins to melt.

Another homely description of surrender is Richard Foster's simple prayer of relinquishment: "How do I give up control? Please, Jesus, teach me your way of relinquishment."

Foster remembers having led a Christian formation group in which a man who was distant from Christianity came to faith. After several sessions of listening, this man asked, "Would you pray for me that I might know Jesus the way you know Jesus?"

After some moments of stunned silence, a young man in the group got up to pray for him. He placed his hands on the man's shoulders and prayed, using an image from a popular Nestea commercial of the day. The image went something like this: People were sitting around in the sweltering sun, longing for relief. The relief provided from drinking the tea was symbolized by various people falling into a swimming pool with a look of "Aaah" on their faces. The young man described this "Aaah" effect, and then prayed that this seeker would know the joy and relief of falling into the arms of Jesus.

Foster asks his readers to cherish this "mental icon" as a way of understanding the prayer of relinquishment.

Sometimes people consider spiritual "surrender" to be a kind of passivity, an admission of defeat. But these examples—and my own experience—suggest otherwise.

Surrender, even a small surrender, is a choice we make for grace. And it is not something we do on our own. It is cooperation with the power of God. Perhaps the best example is that of Jesus in Luke's account of the Garden at Gethsemane. "Then he withdrew from them about a stone's throw, knelt down, and prayed, 'Father, if you are willing, remove this cup from me; yet, not my will but yours be done.'"

Certainly, there are surrenders of momentous proportions, like Jesus' surrender on the cross. But many surrenders are small. When we make them, we are opening ourselves up to God's love, and to our own transformation.

Fifth Sunday Through the Fifth Week of Lent

Fifth Sunday in Lent

*I am the LORD, your Holy One . . . I will make a way in
the wilderness and rivers in the desert . . . to give drink to
my chosen people.*

—Isaiah

ONE OF THE TASKS WE TAKE ON DURING LENT
is to return to God. We want to cross the
distance between God and ourselves. We remember, or think we remember, a time when we were
closer to God. But somehow that conversation
has been broken off.

Why do we drift away from our conversation
with God? One reason we often give is the culture we live in, the people we know, the movies we
see—all those distractions pull us away from the
inward path. But those influences are external;
they affect us, but only when we let them.

Other discouragements may distance us from
God, ones that seem to come from within. Those
are harder to identify and to handle. We imagine
the problem as a shortage of time. "I would pray,

but I can't find the time." Or we find ourselves dealing with low self-esteem, an inner voice that says, "God talks to other people, not to me." Still another obstacle is a kind of un-faith: "Nothing will happen if I pray."

These issues are commonplace. Everybody who attempts a life of prayer experiences one or more of these. They're a nuisance. But at the same time, they're like little weeds in the garden: persistent, but you can deal with them.

Certain other problems in the life of prayer go much deeper. We are less afraid of the prayer in which nothing happens than the prayer in which something happens. We have heard that prayer will change us. Yet we are insecure: do we really want to change? Maybe we have come into the spiritual life with high romantic ideas, but now we are startled by the possibilities. What will God ask of us? Will it stretch us beyond our limits? Thoughts like these make us feel inadequate. We may even begin to wonder about the nature of this relationship. Have our spiritual imaginations gone haywire? What will our friends think of us if we become involved in all this prayer?

As every believing Christian knows, these fears are not completely unfounded. There are precedents for this. Our fear is of a call to follow in the footsteps of Jesus Christ. Our fear is Simon Peter's fear. We are afraid that we will be as faithless as Peter was to Jesus in the Gospel stories, claiming, "I never knew the man. Is he a Galilean? I was never in Galilee."

We know God asks hard things. We are nervous about getting some difficult call. We forget that the people who get those difficult calls are quite able to take them lightly—they are soaked in the grace of God; to do one more thing for him is easy for them. We think how hard this must be, and so we underestimate the power of God's grace. But in Isaiah we find reassurance: "I am the LORD, your Holy One. . . . I will make a way in the wilderness and rivers in the desert . . . to give drink to my chosen people." In our dialogue with God, we must be listeners. We have to trust God to make a way in the wilderness. We have to surrender to God's grace.

Surrender is the essence of our return to God. It is what underlies Christian prayer. Every prayer, any prayer, is really a little surrender. Whether it is the prayer of petition or the prayer of listening, whether it is contemplation or meditation or whatever kind of prayer it is, prayer is surrender.

In returning, we admit that we are not enough for ourselves by ourselves. We bend the knee and say, "My Lord and my God."

Surrender like this exists only in practice. It's not a theory, it's a story. Nobody surrenders by thinking about it. It's not a matter of weighing alternatives, thinking things through. Surrender happens in a particular time and place, in the deserts of our lives, when God lets rivers flow. The Lord, the Holy One, opens the way. And the prodigal son or daughter comes home.

Monday of the Fifth Week

I fled Him, down the nights and down the days;
I fled Him, down the arches of the years. . . .

—Francis Thompson

THE PENITENTIAL SPIRIT OF LENT IS RELATED to what spiritual teachers call the purgative way. This is one of three stages in the spiritual path: the other two are the illuminative and the unitive way.

What is meant by purgation? Sometimes the best way to understand purgation is through someone's story. Take the life of the British poet Francis Thompson. Unlikely though it may seem, one of the great religious poets of the English language was homeless, lived on the streets of London, and was an opium addict for much of his life. That is Francis Thompson's story. However, it is hard to stereotype Thompson as a profligate who lived a life of excess. He was a passionate believer whose sensitive, high-strung nature left him an outsider. And for most of his life he was lost, sick, and destitute.

Thompson was born in Lancashire to devoutly religious Roman Catholic parents. His mother died when he was relatively young, and his father made every effort to see to his education. Thompson first aspired to the priesthood, and studied seven years at Ushaw Seminary, near Durham. Told by the superior that he was not suited to this vocation, he left and attempted to study medicine at Owens College in Manchester. Thompson's father was a doctor, and though the son wanted to follow in his footsteps, he had no liking for medicine. After years of unsuccessful study, he abandoned the medical project and went to London in search of a literary life.

Finally, all his options seemed to vanish, and Thompson lived as a vagrant in extreme poverty. He sold matches and newspapers, received tips for hailing cabs, and was what we would call a panhandler. But somehow, Thompson continued to write poetry that expressed a deep religious vision. Plagued by ill health and emotional dis- affection, he became an opium addict, in an era when laudanum, an opium derivative, was easily obtained over the counter for use as a painkiller.

In spite of his addiction and vagrancy, Thompson was eventually recognized as a remarkable poet by Wilfrid and Alice Meynell, Catholic writers and editors of the publication *Merrie England*. The Meynells published his work, introduced him to other poets, and gave him a home for several years. Today Thompson is best known for "The Hound of Heaven":

I fled Him, down the nights and down the days;
I fled Him, down the arches of the years;
I fled him, down the labyrinthine ways
Of my own mind; and in the mist of tears
I hid from Him, and under running laughter.

"The Hound of Heaven" is one of the great religious love poems. The poem offers a picture of the poet himself in flight from the love of God, with God in hot pursuit. The central metaphor of God as "the hound of heaven" is well known today, far better known than the poem itself. This chase is all about repentance and reconciliation, for Thompson is a prodigal. He needs to forgive himself for the past, for the lost years, the things done wrong and those left undone. But in the end, God's love and forgiveness are enough. God has not waited for the poet to come back to him, but has passionately sought him out and chased him down. God is portrayed as tender in the words he speaks:

> All which I took from Thee I did but take,
> Not only for thy harms,
> But just that Thou might'st seek it in My arms.
> All which thy child's mistake
> Fancies is lost, I have stored for thee at home.

Thompson wrestled throughout his life with his addiction. In his last years he was sick and mentally unbalanced. But he lived in an atmosphere of religious fervor, at religious houses and monasteries in Wales and Storrington. He produced three books of poetry and some important critical essays, and was recognized in literary circles as an original and powerful poet. Thompson's health, never stable, declined sharply in his forties, and he died from tuberculosis.

There is no conventional happy ending in Francis Thompson's life. Even so, we can be grateful for the example of his deep religious faith, and for the power of his poetry. Perhaps his greatest legacy to us is as a spiritual example of one who practiced a continual return to the love and forgiveness of God. Though much of his life seems far from admirable, we admire him. And that is because Thompson's life is all about love. It is all about renunciation and repentance. It is about God pursuing us, even when all seems lost, and gathering us to his wounded heart. And we may ask ourselves: are our own hearts open to such transforming love?

Tuesday of the Fifth Week

Our spiritual formation begins not with fullness, but with emptiness. That's the way we follow Jesus who "emptied himself, taking the form of a slave, being born in human likeness."

—Joshua Choonmin Kang

OUR HOPE, IN LENT, IS TO BREAK THROUGH to another level, a deeper level in the spiritual life. But how? The words of Pastor Joshua Choonmin Kang offer us a clue. We must begin not with fullness but with emptiness.

Kang is the pastor of a large Korean-American church in California. This church is connected to a worldwide Korean ministry. You could call its members Koreans in diaspora, as they are scattered from their old homeland. When my husband and I attend this church, though we speak not a word of Korean, we are moved by the living Spirit of God blowing through this congregation. To hear them speak the name of Jesus—"Jesu! Jesu!"—is very touching.

Pastor Kang teaches that emptiness is the right beginning point in the spiritual life. We must give things up in order to receive Christ. We must set out, as Abraham did, from the old homeland, and go in obedience to God to another place.

This is a moving idea, especially when voiced by Koreans who are far from their native land. But no, the meaning is far beyond geography. Beginning with emptiness means being willing and open to change.

How can I apply this idea—that of beginning with emptiness—to my own life? One of the great changes in my life through the last ten years has been that of aging and disability. But I do not focus on that. At the same time that I am getting older, my writing and speaking have flowered. I have had a deeper sense of calling than ever before. I believe that God is showering me with blessings. Though I can't walk as fast as I used to, and I certainly can't run, I have accepted this diminishment. And oddly, in ways I can't account for, my life has bloomed.

Often the things we give up in Lent are only tokens. In secret, we are holding on for dear life to the things that make us secure: our homes, our community status, our bank accounts. But Jesus calls us to abandon things, to clear space for a new way of living. Are we willing to do this? It is risky, that's for sure.

In the lives of holy people we hear many stories of giving possessions away. Francis of Assisi, we are told, gave up all his clothing—his father was a wealthy merchant—and walked naked through the streets of the town. This makes a good story, but it sounds a bit unbalanced in this day and age.

Jesus told his disciples to drop their nets and follow him, to abandon their fathers and mothers and their wives, not even to pause for such honorable duties as burying their parents. Such radical cases of letting go are well authenticated in Scripture. The trick is to know how to interpret the meaning for our own lives.

Jesus wants us to open our hands and hearts for the grace he will send us. He asks us to examine our dependencies, the things we are attached to. Sometimes these dependencies are so obvious, they're staring us in the face. But sometimes we are blind to the things that drag us down. We are pinned down by our attachments. We think our lives are full, but we're deluding ourselves. The fullness is just an overburdened, complicated life.

Just as Henri Nouwen left Harvard to live with the handicapped, just as Charles Colson left Washington politics to start a prison ministry, just as Mother Teresa left Europe and went to India to serve the poor, we should look for our own points of departure, our emptying. We should not indulge in "copycat" spirituality, trying to do just what Nouwen or Colson or Mother Teresa did. We should reflect on our own lives and let go.

We should shed the attachments that pin us down and hem us in. Nobody else knows what they are quite as well as we do.

These are the secrets of the spiritual life: letting go, relinquishing, emptying ourselves, so that our hearts can be made full and whole.

Wednesday of the Fifth Week

A moderate amount of anxiety seems to be a necessary stimulus for growth and development; if we never experienced novelty, we would never change.

—William A. Barry and William J. Connolly

ONE WAY WE REFLECT ON OUR LIVES DURING Lent is by examining our life choices. Every time you make a choice, you are opting for something that will change or transform you. You are becoming better or worse, choosing to live more generously or more selfishly. A moral dimension is involved.

When I think about my own life choices, I remember a critical year: age nineteen. I was in college, but I could see my student days coming to an end. Now I had to decide about my life's work. Possibly that was the first year I began making my own choices instead of having the system, or parental figures, make them for me. What was the big issue? Choosing my life's work turned out to be an uncomfortable process, with many factors I couldn't predict or control. When

I did make my move—out of the university, into the marketplace—I felt the pain of it. But I also felt a sense of resolution.

One of the most important factors in our choosing is love. When we choose our work, or a mate, or allegiances—to a cause or to an enterprise, when we choose God, love is what drives us. One of my choices was to leave my home in New Orleans and go to New York City. When I did that, New York looked like an enchanted place, a Jerusalem far off, where all opportunities were possible. But when I was actually in my city of desire, I saw that it could become, and did become, a city of disenchantment.

In the middle of that time, I began to long for something or someone beyond the ordinary run of friends and companions, beyond the ebb and flow and disappointment of daily life. I wanted someone I could always believe in, someone whose love I could depend on, whose affections would not blow hot and cold.

But wanting to believe in God, even being sure that such a being is possible, is still a long way from choosing to belong to God. This is the passage I eventually made. Not all at once, but in fits and starts, by a kind of wrestling and running away from the demands of such a mighty Love. Not surprisingly, I wanted to know how other people had dealt with such questions. I began to read first-person accounts mostly by people in my own time, a generation or so ahead of me.

There was a college student named Thomas Merton, who had knocked around in a lot of places in Europe, who had studied at Cambridge University in England and at Columbia University in New York, and who, when he eventually came to God, made a radical decision to become a man of prayer, in a Trappist monastery in Kentucky.... I would sit in my office on the thirty-seventh floor of the Tishman Building in New York City, and when I had a few minutes left over, I would snitch another few pages of this book, and was amazed because Merton had felt what I felt: alienation, disenchantment, longing . . . and that had led him to God.

There was also another New Yorker, a young journalist named Dorothy Day. She was living with a man named Forster who didn't believe in

God. And she was carrying his child. Her pregnancy brought her to God. She was glad to be pregnant. She started thinking about Bible people like Mary and Elizabeth, who were so glad to be pregnant. Dorothy Day started a garden. And she kept on pondering these things in her heart. Forster kept telling her there wasn't any God. But then one day when she was spading the earth, she said out loud, "How can there be no God when there are all these beautiful things?"

When she chose God, she broke away from Forster. He couldn't accept her belief in God. But this was a decision made for love. Not only love of God, but love for the child who was going to be born.

Some of these events I have mentioned were dramatic. But some were small. If you blinked, you would hardly notice them. Yet these little events were magnified by the person's need for God. Our longing for God is enormous. We need the love of God, to be rescued and saved, to know about resurrection and joy. This is a lovely combination: great longings and small surrenders. This is the kind of choosing that transforms us.

Thursday of the Fifth Week

But there are also many other things that Jesus did; if every one of them were written down, I suppose that the world itself could not contain the books that would be written.

—John

IT IS A CREATIVE EXERCISE TO CONSTANTLY renew and refresh my mental picture of Jesus. I see others doing this as well. It is also a spiritual exercise, one that keeps us limber in the spiritual life.

One of my daughters is a portrait artist. Recently I attended a demonstration she gave and watched her paint a portrait from life, explaining her method all the while. On other occasions I have heard her talk about times when one must work from photographs. Then, when the finished portrait appears, one listens to the reactions. "Oh, it is just like him." "It really captures his personality."

Books, plays, and films about Jesus can be useful to "capture" him. These mental portraits painted by others are assembled from various sources and insights. They help us to see Jesus, to keep our relationship fresh. When we engage with creative works, there may be some elements in them that don't work for us, that we disregard or discard. But even this exercise, that of critically examining another person's picture of Jesus, is the way that we paint portraits of our own.

Dallas Willard sketches valuable pictures of Jesus in his books *The Divine Conspiracy* and *The Renovation of the Heart*. Each book is a careful reconstruction of Jesus' teaching, getting to the heart of what Jesus has to say. When you read them, you feel you are getting to know Jesus better. *The Jesus Way*, by Eugene H. Peterson, captures Jesus vividly so that we can again begin to learn from him.

Garry Wills has recently written a book called *What Jesus Meant*. He calls it a devotional work, one in which he wants to bring Jesus closer for himself. What intrigues me about this book is not so much his picture of Jesus, as how he develops the picture—his method, if you will. I watch him sorting through the ways that other individuals (Thomas Jefferson, for one) have tried to domesticate Jesus. He rejects those domestications. He sorts through some conclusions of modern scholars and discards them. He then reads the Gospels for himself, trying to synthesize the four Gospel portraits, finding the parallels and differences among these different pictures of Jesus. He brings in knowledge from other sources, knowledge of the ancient world, and makes educated guesses. From time to time he brings in the writings of St. Paul.

Wills is trying to restore a vivid picture of Jesus for himself, one that will have coherence for him. While I do not agree with all of his conclusions, Wills offers me a vigorous encounter with Jesus, and I come away with my own Jesus portrait revitalized and fresh.

When C.S. Lewis wrote *The Chronicles of Narnia* he recast the Gospel stories in a mythological framework. He too was refreshing his own image of Jesus. Reflecting on his own efforts to recover a vital Christian faith, he had an insight: "But supposing that by casting all these things into an imaginary world, stripping them of their stained-glass and Sunday School associations, one could make them for the first time appear in their real potency? Could one not thus steal past those watchful dragons? I thought one could." Aslan, the lion-messiah, becomes Lewis's way to refresh the picture of Jesus in his own mind and heart. I think many religious writers and creative artists are driven by this personal desire.

In what way, then, does this process converge with our Lenten surrender? Reimagining Jesus can be one way we give ourselves to him, a vital part of our desire to know Jesus, to talk and walk with him.

Friday of the Fifth Week

When we suffer these things—things for which we are not responsible and over which we have no control—we are to endure them patiently, putting our trust in God.

—Richard J. Foster

Fridays in Lent are good days to recall the sufferings of the Lord. We don't do that to mire ourselves in sadness. We do it instead to bear our own sufferings well.

When people think of the sufferings of Jesus, they usually remember his suffering on the cross. This is understandable. However, it might be worthwhile to remember another way that Jesus suffered. That was by rejection. In the Gospel of Luke we find him reproaching those towns and communities who rejected his teaching: "Woe to you, Chorazin! Woe to you, Bethsaida! For if the deeds of power done in you had been done in Tyre and Sidon, they would have repented long ago, sitting in sackcloth and ashes."

Throughout the Gospels we see that Jesus' words and actions were upsetting to people. They got riled about him. They challenged him. The Gospel of John records such challenges: "How can this man give us his flesh to eat?" And in one case it is noted that they "no longer went about with him."

Disputes arose among his followers after Jesus gave his teaching on the Eucharist. He described his own flesh as the bread that came down from heaven. "Those who eat my flesh and drink my blood abide in me, and I in them. . . . The one who eats this bread will live for ever."

After hearing these claims, some disciples deserted him, and Jesus asked of those who remained, "Do you also wish to go away?" Simon Peter, speaking for the Twelve, said they would be faithful.

Jesus knew that many people hated him and wanted to kill him, and he knew their reasons. He foresaw his own suffering yet to come. When he sent his disciples out, he warned them about rejection. And he also taught that such rejection would be a blessing: "Blessed are those who are persecuted for righteousness' sake. . . . Blessed are you when people revile you and persecute you and utter all kinds of evil against you falsely on my account. Rejoice and be glad. . . ." These words from the Sermon on the Mount, in Matthew's Gospel, make sense in the context of what Jesus endured.

It is a Christian teaching to rejoice in suffering. In the letter of James we read, "Whenever you face trials of any kind, consider it nothing but joy." James says this testing of our faith brings us to full maturity.

As difficult or unlikely as it seems, we are encouraged as Christian believers to enter into this maturity on purpose. We do this by a kind of inner drama: we join our sufferings to those of the Lord, who is infinitely more able than we are to bear them.

This spiritual exercise is sometimes described as a joining. We join our sufferings to those of Jesus. We do not want suffering, but when sufferings come, we take them to the Lord.

The mystery of Jesus as both God and man is that he suffers deeply, humanly. He feels the rejection of cities and towns like Chorazin and Bethsaida. He is conscious of the rejection of those who no longer go about with him. He is afraid of those who are plotting against his life and he takes precautions to avoid them. He is conscious of the evil in the world.

The sacrifice and redemption of Jesus Christ stand in the gap, weigh on the balance against all human suffering.

The spiritual writer Richard Foster counsels us to practice the prayer of suffering. Sometimes it is a prayer of repentance for our own wrongdoing. Sometimes it is a prayer of trust in God when unjust sufferings have come our way. Sometimes it is a prayer to take on the sufferings of others, and by our prayer, to relieve them. By this kind of prayer we may even embrace the sufferings of the world, the wars, the famines, the ethnic cleansings, the suicide bombings, the persecutions. We give them to Jesus. We give them to God.

When we join our sufferings and those of others to the sufferings of Jesus, something will come right.

We know that God desires the healing of the world. He will dry every tear. He will lift our sorrows. He will use our sorrows. When we join our sufferings to those of the Son, we will come by a mystery into joy.

This kind of prayer is a wrestling with the mystery of evil. In this prayer we acknowledge what we do not understand—in our own lives, in the sorrow of the world—and we lift it up to God.

The Christian religion asks us to put our trust not in ideas, and certainly not in ideologies, but in a God who was vulnerable enough to become human and die, and who desires to be present to us in our ordinary circumstances.

—Kathleen Norris

SOMEHOW, WHERE SPIRITUAL LIFE IS concerned, we long for exalted circumstances. On some level we suppose that since God is exalted, we too must become exalted in order to converse with him. We fantasize about mystical life and mountaintop experiences. But most of the Christian stories give scant support for this. In the Gospels at least, Jesus appears in ordinary circumstances. He is visiting Martha and Mary at their home in Bethany. He is walking along the roads, going from town to town. He is on the shores of Galilee with his friends, or crossing the water in a fishing boat.

The parables Jesus teaches are filled with metaphors from ordinary experience. A sower went out to sow . . . the tares and the wheat will grow together until the harvest. . . . Even after his resurrection he is still operating in terms of the ordinary. To prove to the disciples that he is not a ghost but resurrected in his body, he asks for a piece of fish and eats it right in front of them.

One great teacher of the prayer of the ordinary was Thérèse Martin, better known as Thérèse of Lisieux or "The Little Flower." Thérèse, who came from a devout French family, entered the convent in her teens and died in her mid-twenties, but became known for an earthy kind of devotion called "The Little Way." Therese did not become well known until after her death, but then, through her spiritual autobiography, she became world famous. "The Little Way" became popular as a spirituality of ordinary circumstances.

Thérèse certainly began in the spiritual life with noble aspirations and the desire for romantic deeds of love like martyrdom, something that for a French child of her era would have been much idealized. But as she grew in spiritual life, she aspired to such things less and less. What she wanted was to express love and devotion in the smallest ways, by a look, a glance, a helpful action. She is often cited as one who understood how to pray in the middle of ordinary domestic work, folding laundry, mending, sewing, embroidering. She felt that great deeds were beyond her, that she did not have the intellect or the education for scholarly reflection and study. Nevertheless, she loved the Bible and found that Bible stories and phrases opened up a whole universe.

Thérèse's view was that love shows itself by deeds, and the deeds she could perform were small, loving ones. She referred to these loving deeds as "scattered flowers," from which her nickname, "The Little Flower," was taken.

Thérèse is generally thought to be a mystic, but she did not consider herself to be exalted in prayer. She imagined herself serving Jesus through modest sacrifices and surrenders, doing little actions for love.

How can we appropriate this close-to-the-ground spirituality? First of all, we can see the ordinary, menial tasks as a way of knowing Jesus, "the God who desires to be present to us in ordinary circumstances." Instead of insisting on privileges and preferments, we can accept simple and humble tasks as a way of coming closer to him.

During my most intense years in the business world (writing, telephoning, traveling, meeting, negotiating), I often found myself exhausted on Saturdays, with nothing in front of me but a mess of domestic chores. But as I performed them, without much ardor, I began to see that the very slowness of these chores could become a gift of grace. They reminded me of the prayer I should have been praying: *Slow me down, Lord!* Often I forgot the importance of slowing down. The restorative power of domestic chores, a kind of remedy for stress, took me by surprise.

Esther de Waal, a writer, teacher, and fine interpreter of Benedictine simplicity, loves to remind us of the Benedictine interweaving of work and prayer. She speaks ardently of the prayers that accompany manual labor: the prayers of the loom, of the mending of the nets, of the teakettle. (One's prayer could rise with the steam, as prayers rise like incense in the psalms.) At a workshop I once asked de Waal if one could also pray with electric teakettles. She assured me that one could. (I was trying to decide whether high-technology work was also congenial to prayer.)

Lent gives us many opportunities for prayer that is low to the ground, simple, little, and ordinary. We can know Jesus in the midst of ordinary life, if we remember that such a thing is possible.

Palm Sunday Through Easter Sunday

Sixth Sunday in Lent: Palm Sunday

Monday in Holy Week

Tuesday in Holy Week

Wednesday in Holy Week

Holy Thursday

Good Friday

Holy Saturday

Easter Sunday

Sixth Sunday in Lent: Palm Sunday

The pilgrims covered the eighty-eight miles from Nazareth to Jerusalem in four days. As they passed through the changing landscape they filled the hours with blessings, prayers and reflections on the destiny of Israel.

—Robert Aron

A FRIEND OF MINE TOLD ME ABOUT A HOMILY that moved him, given by a man who, facing a terminal illness himself, spoke about Jesus walking to Jerusalem. And the repeated thought, the refrain of it was: "He kept on walking."

During the last week of Lent we focus on the constancy of Jesus. We know that Jesus has prepared himself by a time of trial in the wilderness. We know that he must endure a still greater trial. In this week that we call Holy Week, we relive the last week of Jesus' life: his entrance into Jerusalem, his Passover meal, his arrest, interrogation, suffering, and death.

In Jesus' time, pilgrimages to the Holy City were a regular part of Jewish life. According to law, every Jewish male was obligated to go to the temple three times a year. Passover was one of these times. Inns and stopping points along the road catered to pilgrims on their journey. Jerusalem would be overflowing when Jesus and his entourage arrived. Flavius Josephus, fifty years later, estimated the Passover crowds at two and a half million to three million for a city of only 250,000 permanent residents. Perhaps his figures are inflated. But as we imagine that first Palm Sunday, we see that many thousands were on hand for Passover, and Jesus was by no means the center of attention.

But now he is our center of attention. As we try to recapture him, to bring him closer to us, we find him continuing his pilgrimage. Mostly he is walking. As Mark's Gospel tells us, "They were on the road, going up to Jerusalem, and Jesus was walking ahead of them; they were amazed, and those who followed were afraid. He took the twelve aside again and began to tell them what was to happen to him."

Christians believe that Jesus, through his privileged divine identity, had foresight. He had more than a premonition. He knew how the story would unfold. But he did not give up, he did not run away, he did not despair. Although most of the time Jesus had tried to avoid the limelight and the huzzahs of the crowd, as he entered Jerusalem he accepted a bit of celebrity. He continued on the path.

He sent others to prepare the Feast of the Passover. They had to hire a room, arrange for the meal, decide who the guests would be. A terrible ordeal lay ahead. Jesus would have to deal with being brought before the Sanhedrin, with unjust arrest by the Roman soldiers, with scourging, with execution. He knew all that, but he kept on walking.

He had to deal with the false encouragement of his own disciples. One of them would betray him. Others, like Peter, who meant to be stead-fast, couldn't take the pressure. The disciples really didn't understand. Jesus found himself more and more alone. But he kept on walking.

When my friend heard this sermon preached, he was struck by the parallels in our own lives. His friend, the homilist, knew his own life was ending. As he spoke about the last days of Jesus, the meaning was clear. Jesus kept on walking.

At the same time, Jesus was choosing. He wasn't being passively dragged forward by circumstances. He had options, ways of eluding the evident conspiracy, the sentence of death. But Jesus knew and understood more than anyone around him. He had a sense of God's larger plan. He saw what his short life story was about. And he *chose* to embrace the path ahead.

Two thousand years later, the ancient story moves us. No matter how often we hear it, it stirs up another meaning. Sometimes this Passover time may coincide with some life crisis of our own. Sometimes Holy Week comes at a flat and restless time. Often, in the rush of Easter preparation we are tempted to overlook the sacred message.

But Jesus kept on walking. Among the crowds in Jerusalem who did not know him, among the people who wanted to shower him with celebrity status, among his friends who had only a dim idea, even in his dialogue with Pilate, Jesus continued. He did all these things for us, long before we were born.

What does the death of someone who lived and died two thousand years ago have to do with us? It is not just a case of perseverance, or human courage. It is far more than a great moral example. This drama of reconciliation is a turning point in human history, as decisive as Abraham and Isaac, Moses and the Israelites. It is a story we can barely grasp, yet it is meant for us. The story draws us in. We keep on walking.

Monday in Holy Week

Christ is still a pilgrim, traveling inside a paradox Peter could not fathom: a man going to his destiny, yet already in the Heart of Destiny.

—Paul Marechal

EACH FAITHFUL CHRISTIAN HAS A CONSTANTLY developing personal picture of Jesus as both man and God. We sit in church week after week, hearing the words and actions of Jesus in the Gospel readings. Sometimes we envision a scene: Jesus telling a story, Jesus healing an invalid, Jesus befriending an outcast, Jesus holding his own against a scribe or a Pharisee. In the epistles we get another vantage point on who Jesus is and what we should believe about him. In our devotional lives we turn to Jesus; in doing so, we gain a mind's eye picture of him. It's important in our devotional lives to keep the picture constantly fresh, through devotional readings, works of art, plays, and films.

What is Jesus really like? Theologians and scholars distinguish between a high and a low

Christology (a technical term for knowledge of the Christ). They also speak of a Christology as "ascending" or "descending." By and large this is about a difference of emphasis. An ascending Christology begins from the humanity of Jesus and moves upward. The Gospel of Mark is a good example of such a representation. The Gospel of John, by contrast, reflects a high Christology, focusing on Jesus' divinity. Each one of the four Gospels, though they differ in some details, is giving us a portrait of the same individual. Theology studies try to sharpen the picture of Christ that emerges. But meantime, the first-year theology student is wrestling with technical terms that are new and strange. The person in the pew may never hear these terms at all.

When I studied theology, I realized that believers who profess the same creed may hold "lower" or "higher" Christologies, for many reasons. Our devotional lives shape us. We may be more inclined to literal or figurative biblical interpretation. We may be struggling to reconcile the miracle stories of the Gospels with our own understanding of scientific realities. We are reaching for an adequate understanding of who Jesus is, what he does, and what he means for us.

Grappling with these issues, I once blurted out in class, "Well, what about those words in today's preface?" I went on to quote one of the Easter prefaces, which had been recited in church that day: *In him a new age has dawned / the long reign of sin has ended / a broken world has been renewed / and man is once again made whole.* My professor may have thought I was putting him on the spot, though I was the one on the spot. "That's poetry," he coolly replied.

Now and then I read a new interpretation of Jesus by a contemporary scholar. Even when I don't agree with every theory or speculation, my picture of Jesus is sharpened. I see him. He walks ahead of me. *Ecce homo.* There is the man.

Year by year the picture develops. The perspective lengthens. Perhaps I now see Jesus in a more rounded way than I could in earlier days. More and more I am drawn to the mystical writers and the way they depict Jesus for me.

Paul Marechal, a Cistercian brother, has written a brief but profoundly mystical book that speaks to my heart. In it he locates Jesus within the tradition of pilgrimage:

> Jesus was another pilgrim: a luminous being who roamed inside the lowlands of the friends and the friendless, and in the back country of the washed and unwashed. With no place to lay his head, everyone was his refuge, every place his home.

Was Jesus actually homeless? Perhaps. Scholars differ about this. But Marechal is spinning out a high Christology in which the "homelessness" of Jesus frees him from the ordinary demands of living and puts him into constant pilgrimage. In the Gospel of John, Simon Peter sees his teacher's pilgrimage but can only partly understand it. He wants to follow, but Jesus says he can't, not just yet. "Where I am going, you cannot follow me now; but you will follow afterward."

Like many others before him, Marechal is writing his own gospel. It is one that touches me. Marechal doesn't speak of Jesus as making this or that pilgrimage. He sees his whole life as pilgrimage. For him, Christ is a pilgrim "traveling inside a paradox Peter could not fathom."

Sometimes it takes a poetic insight to grasp the mystery of Jesus living and dying: a man going to his destiny, yet already in the heart of destiny.

Then he said to them all, "If any want to become my followers, let them deny themselves and take up their cross daily and follow me."

—Luke

THIS SAYING OF JESUS (ATTRIBUTED TO HIM by Matthew, Mark, and Luke) baffled me for a long time. It is a saying that has to be translated into everyday life. Denying oneself is an easy enough notion, though sometimes hard to apply. But taking up my cross? I sometimes thought of this expression as melodramatic, self-conscious. It wasn't an expression you could use in ordinary conversation.

Over time I began to interpret taking up the cross in terms of acceptance and surrender. A woman I know has been diagnosed with Alzheimer's disease. Thanks to her attentive daughter, she continues to appear at social events. When this woman sees me, she beams. But I am fairly sure she can't remember my name. This diagnosis is her cross and her family's, but it is also mine. Her limitations remind me of my own.

More recently I have heard the same diagnosis for a literary scholar I know. He is some ten years younger than I. We have been friends for decades. I am shocked to learn that he is battling this disease, that he has contracted it so early. But my faith requires of me that I accept this blow with equanimity. It is one of my small, or not-so-small surrenders.

The friend who calls to tell me about this man's illness is saddened to give me such news so close to Easter. But what better time? Lent is a time of surrendering our will to God's. It is also a time of believing in a better outcome yet to come.

In Holy Week I find myself remembering good friends and loved ones who have died. I am hemmed in by these losses and these memories. I have lost three, four, no, five of my close contemporaries.

> They are all gone into the world of light
> And I alone sit lingering here.
> Their very memory is fair and bright,
> And my sad thoughts doth clear.

The poem by Henry Vaughan is embedded in my memory. How well it expresses the loss of my own close friends. Henry Vaughan lived in the seventeenth century, when seventy-three was a ripe old age. But his feelings about the loss of friends are just like mine.

One way we surrender is by letting our friends go ahead of us into the world of light. I compare notes with my husband, who remembers these friends as well. These people are still alive, not only in God's heart but in our hearts. We recall them vividly. We reconstruct and reenact past conversations with them, happy occasions all. We tell funny stories and quote their best punch lines. They are alive to us. But they are gone.

> I see them walking in an air of glory
> Whose light doth trample on my days;
> My days, which are at best but dull and hoary,
> Mere glimmering and decays.

Henry Vaughan has the advantage over me in dealing with his losses. He has a vivid imagination of heaven, richer than any mind picture I can see. He sees his friends walking in an air of glory, of celestial light. I want to recover this lively faith, this rich vision of the life to come. Vaughan speaks of "holy hope" and "high humility" that come to help him kindle his cold love. Do I need hotter love to bridge the imaginative gap? I name the friends I have lost. I release them to God. Then I think of Jesus' Transfiguration, which bridges me over to the world of light.

Six days later, Jesus took with him Peter and James and his brother John and led them up a high mountain, by themselves. And he was transfigured before them, and his face shone like the sun, and his clothes became dazzling white. Suddenly there appeared to them Moses and Elijah, talking with him.

In Matthew's Gospel, as they were coming down the mountain, Jesus ordered them, "Tell no one about the vision until after the Son of Man has been raised from the dead."

Not everyone receives a vision of the trans-figured Jesus, talking with Moses and Elijah, to bridge the gap into glory. But in order to take up the cross daily, we need such vividly imaginative faith. Accepting, for example, the death of friends is eased when we can imagine them going before us into God's light. Imaginative faith can transfigure our daily lives and help us to make our small and large surrenders.

Wednesday in Holy Week

Let him easter in us,
be a dayspring to the dimness in us
— Gerard Manley Hopkins

I REMEMBER A STORY IN THE *NEW YORK TIMES* about the Robinson family in Violet, Louisiana. They were living in the middle of a desolate stretch in St. Bernard Parish, one of the sections hardest hit by Hurricane Katrina. Their blue house with white trim was uninhabitable. But the Robinsons had come back to lot number 6429, beginning life again in a government-issued trailer. A forty-five-minute drive to the Wal-Mart in Gretna was their best option for grocery shopping. Mail service was lacking. Electricity was scarce. Nothing remained of their former civilization except their cell phones and church.

Amazingly, they were not alone. Some eight thousand people of the former seventy thousand had returned to repopulate St. Bernard Parish. Their future was uncertain. They had little guidance for cleaning, gutting, or rebuilding their homes. They were trying to rebuild on their own. They gathered to remember times past. They took note of four hundred dollars' worth of shrimp in the freezer that had been lost when Katrina came through. It was more than just the loss of food. That shrimp, stored for an upcoming party, symbolized a spirit of celebration. For these are celebrating people, people who love a good time.

As neighbors—their names are Brunet, Dauterive, Napolitano—all were mourning for the sense of community they once had. They came close to tears when they remembered the pre-hurricane times. Their lives had been swept away. Bryan Brunet remembered the house he had built from scratch, the wiring, the contracting. He knew he could do it again. But would the government support his desire to return? Would other neighbors return? Would the effort be worthwhile?

These hurricane-struck people in St. Bernard Parish had no clear vision about the future. But even when things looked impossible, they stayed put. They held on. They clung to some sense of recovery, some glimpse of restoration. They set their hearts on rebuilding; they dreamed; they planned. They were people of hope.

Hope is not certainty. Hope is not settled cheerfulness. Hope is sometimes described as "hope against hope."

When I think of the way Christ redeems us, I think of people like these, people who are making a recovery. "Let him easter in us," wrote Gerard Manley Hopkins in his poem *The Wreck of the Deutschland*. In this case, "easter" is a nautical term. It means steering our craft towards the east, into the light. Throughout the forty days of Lent we have been heading toward the light, trying to shake the darkness, the doubts, the burdens of living, the heaviness of heart. By walking with Christ, letting him easter in us, we mean to turn in the right direction.

But some of our burdens are not so easily shed. I deal with a chronic illness: my hands are cramped by arthritis; I can't walk as far as I once did; I rely on a cane; I depend on the kindness of others. Though I continue to work, write, and travel, I sense my limits.

One way I can respond to this is by taking a downward spiral, saying everything is going straight to hell. Anxiety escalates. Left unchecked, it rockets out of control.

Hopkins knew about this. He was a man plagued by frailty and weakness, not just physical but psychological. At times he would plummet into an abyss of darkness, what he called "cliffs of fall." The steep dropping-off places of the soul seemed worse than any physical distress. This, therefore, was Hopkins's prayer, his hope: "Let him easter in us, be a dayspring to the dimness of us."

What will divert me from that downward spiral, those cliffs of fall?

In his writings, St. Paul makes an extraordinary claim, repeated at least fifty times, that we are in Christ. When I let Christ easter in me, I am changed in ways I don't fully understand. Christ in me can transform my attitude and give me a simpler outlook, a more childlike hope. Something—I think it is grace—brings me into the garden with Jesus. It is Christ who comes to Easter in me.

When Gerard Manley Hopkins wrote his poem, he was dealing with a disaster that completely baffled him. He dedicated his poem to the memory of five Franciscan nuns drowned between midnight and morning of December 8, 1875, when the German ship *Deutschland* went down. He says theirs is a happy memory, but that is a convention in speaking of the dead. Really what he says in the poem is that God is beyond our grasp. Hopkins's prayer is about a disaster he could not interpret or explain. His expression of faith still moves us today.

He prays that Christ will easter in us, be a dayspring to the dimness of us. As we confront the challenges of our lives, there is bad news all around us. But we can let the good news transform us: that God is our security and our hope.

The Eucharist is far more than just a meal; it has cost a death to provide it, and the majesty of death is present in it. Whenever we hold it, we should be filled with reverence in the face of this mystery, with awe in the face of this mysterious death that becomes a present reality in our midst.

—Pope Benedict XVI

HOLY THURSDAY REENACTS THE LAST meal Jesus ate with his disciples. It was the Passover meal. On the rare occasions when I have been invited to a Passover meal in a Jewish home, I have felt a special kind of reverence. There is a connection between Jews and Christians. We do not hold the same beliefs about Jesus, but we understand and honor each other's traditions.

I had a similar experience during an ecumenical Christian conference held in Elizabethtown, Pennsylvania. One of the hosts for the conference, who came from an Anabaptist tradition, told me that in his church they practice the washing of the feet. He showed me the basin and the towel they use. Again, I felt a sense of connection, for this ritual is practiced in Roman Catholic churches every Holy Thursday. Twelve people sit near the altar, representing Jesus' twelve disciples. The celebrant, taking a basin and a towel, goes to each one and washes his or her feet. It is a touching reenactment of the way Jesus behaved with the twelve disciples at the Last Supper.

A more ancient name for this day is Maundy Thursday, and some churches continue to call it by this name. It is thought that the word "Maundy" comes from the Latin word *mandatum*, meaning "mandate" or "command." As part of the liturgy we are instructed to wash one another's feet. It is the Lord's command.

Once, when I took part in this ritual, I realized I was ashamed of my feet. They were somewhat misshapen, nothing to be proud of. It felt strange to have someone else washing them. I understood Peter's resistance. But Jesus was adamant about this. "Peter said to him, 'You will never wash my feet.' Jesus answered, 'Unless I wash you, you have no share with me.' Simon Peter said to him, 'Lord, not my feet only but also my hands and my head!'"

Even more affecting is the institution of the Eucharist on this day. As Pope Benedict says, it is far more than a meal. We are awed when we approach this sacrament, to celebrate it, to distribute it, to receive it. At various times in my church life I have served as a minister of the Eucharist. This is an amazing form of service, one that brings us closer to the sacred event we commemorate. This circle of flat white bread we hold in our hands, this cup we sip, these have become for us the sacred body and blood of the Lord. The whole fabric of the Church, its far-flung work throughout the world, its constantly repeated words of prayer and blessing, all these flow in some sense from this one event, when Jesus and his disciples were together for a final meal.

The Eucharist is far more than just a meal; it has cost a death to provide it, and the majesty of death is present in it. Pope Benedict says that the majesty of death is present in the Eucharistic feast. It is a mystery beyond our comprehension, but one that we continually celebrate.

On the night he was betrayed, he took bread in his sacred hands, and when he had given thanks. . . . The words of the consecration are embedded in our hearts. We believe that when we come to take part in this sacred meal, we become one body, a Church. We are joined to each other in a mystery that blesses and transforms us. It is a mystery that is invisibly transforming the world.

While they were eating, Jesus took a loaf of bread, and after blessing it he broke it, gave it to the disciples, and said, "Take, eat; this is my body." Then he took a cup, and after giving thanks he gave it to them, saying, "Drink from it, all of you; for this is my blood of the covenant, which is poured out for many for the forgiveness of sins. I tell you, I will never again drink of this fruit of the vine until that day when I drink it new with you in my Father's kingdom."

On this day we honor in a special way the Eucharist that transforms us every day of the year. With every Eucharist we are plunged into the mystery of Christ's death, a death that gives life. This is a mystery that becomes real every Holy Thursday, and every Eucharist of our lives.

Good Friday

Could I behold those hands, which span the poles
and tune all spheres at once, pierced with those holes?
—John Donne

OFTEN I FIND MYSELF ON GOOD FRIDAY doing the busy things that work and family life demand, but wishing I could be entirely with the Lord. The streets are choked with traffic. The stores are jammed with busy people, planning Easter baskets and buying food for Easter dinners. Parties and Easter egg hunts have been arranged. Everything is in full swing.

I take part in all this, but on another level my thoughts are somewhere else. Then I remember John Donne's touching meditation in his poem, "Good Friday, 1613: Riding Westward." A few hundred years before me, he had similar thoughts and feelings on Good Friday. He was riding westward when he should be turning eastward, toward Jerusalem, toward Calvary.

Donne was reflecting on the global consequences of Christ's crucifixion, death, and resurrection.

But that Christ on his cross did rise and fall,
Sin had eternally benighted all.

All my life, it seems, I have been feeling this tension. I remember desperate moments when my children were young and I was full of religious zeal, wanting to go to Good Friday and Easter Vigil services, but unable to arrange it. I was on duty. On the home front I was in charge. How was it that the greatest event in history was being commemorated, and I was somewhere else? But my life was full of conflicts. I had obligations.

The answer, of course, is in the interior gaze. Jesus is present to us when we are present to him, and that can be anywhere, whether we are riding eastward or westward.

We can think of him when we are stuck in grocery lines and traffic jams.

Of course, it is more consoling when we are in church, encouraged by images of the crucifix and by stained-glass windows with the sun streaming through.

But the crucifixion of Jesus is a universal fact. It took place once and forever. In the religious imagination it takes place everywhere.

Donne says he is almost glad that he was not present on the day Jesus was crucified.

> Yet dare I almost be glad, I do not see
> That spectacle of too much weight for me....
> What a death were it then to see God die?

Yet we should place ourselves in the scene on Calvary, to imagine, to the extent that we can tolerate it, what happened there.

Donne, in his poetic meditation, imagines the cosmic reality of the crucifixion. Countless criminals were executed by the Roman authorities in this way, a hideous and painful death. But Donne projects this one crucifixion as having endless height, being "zenith to us and our antipodes." He cannot visualize it; he cannot comprehend it. He tries to imagine the flesh of Jesus ragged and torn. He doesn't dare look at this hateful scene.

All forms of torture and execution are hideous. But Jesus' crucifixion was more than a public execution. When we contemplate the crucifixion of

Jesus, we need to focus not only on the pain and humiliation, but on a broader meaning.

When Jesus was put to death, he accepted that death. He gave his life for the sake of his friends. We are included in that generous gift. He gave his life for us.

How can I comprehend this mystery? I am in debt to Jesus for something that happened long ago, not only my redemption but the redemption of the whole world.

It is a loving act, a reconciliation.

Even more than that: Christians believe that the dying and the rising are linked; they are part of the same wonderful event that Jesus promised: "Destroy this temple, and in three days I will raise it up."

Why is it that the principal event of Christianity is the crucifixion? Why is the cross our major symbol? Death is the central mystery, the bafflement that makes us most afraid.

But Jesus, the Messiah, was willing to die for our sakes. His dying set us free.

We have heard it over and over, yet we can barely grasp it.

Next, Donne looks at the sorrowful mother
standing at the foot of the cross:

> If on these things I durst not look,
> durst I
> On his distressed Mother cast mine eye,
> Who was God's partner here, and furnished thus
> Half of that sacrifice which ransomed us?

In adding Jesus' mother to the scene, John
Donne heightens the pressure. Standing at the
foot of the cross, she represents all of humanity
and Donne himself. She represents us.

What is Donne's prayer? For him, the gaze of
Jesus from the cross prompts a desire to be transformed. It is a fine Good Friday prayer.

> Burn off my rust, and my deformity;
> Restore Thine image, so much, by
> Thy grace,
> That Thou mayst know me, and I'll
> turn my face.

If we have learned to encounter others based on a genuine communion with God, we can truly love those whom we do not like or even know. We become capable of looking at them from the perspective of Jesus Christ and, as it were, with his eyes.

—Avery Cardinal Dulles

HOW HARD DO WE TRY TO FORGIVE OUR enemies? The way Jesus forgave his enemies from the cross? As we move from Good Friday to Easter Sunday, we can reflect on what it really means to imitate Christ.

On September 13, 2001, two days after the terrorist attacks on the United States, I was listening to the measured voices of National Public Radio when I heard an interview with a British journalist stationed in the Middle East. In answer to questions from the NPR interviewer, he was attempting to explain Osama bin Laden.

I found myself totally attentive. By now, like most of the nation, I was convinced that bin Laden had inspired, if not directed, these attacks. Something in me wanted to understand this elusive figure. The British journalist, who had interviewed bin Laden during the nineties, made clear one salient thing. Bin Laden did not appropriate the title of "terrorist." No. Instead, he saw himself as a man of the highest moral vision, embracing poverty, fighting for the liberty of his country, doing the will of God as he understood it. In an effort to explain the deep asceticism of his commitment, bin Laden called attention to his own radically poor way of living. He insisted that the journalist also visit his three wives, who lived as simply as he. If fighting for the liberty of one's country was terrorism, bin Laden would accept the title, he said. But his goal was to liberate his citizens from the evil of American influence in Islamic lands.

The text about loving your enemies came to mind. If I was obliged to love bin Laden, was I also obliged to embrace his worldview, to sympathize with his hatred for the United States, to suppose that there must be a reason why he has called for the death of all Americans?

Do we have heroes in our own tradition who are essentially outlaws and terrorists? Surely Robin Hood, with his gang of outlaws, gratuitously attacked the rich in order to help the poor. In Louisiana, the Pirate Jean Lafitte always enjoyed enormous popularity. His acts of piracy were considered romantic, and he gained a popular following against the unromantic governor of Louisiana who put a price on his head.

But hard as I tried, the figure of Osama bin Laden seemed closer to that of Adolf Hitler than to any other leader I could think of. The deep economic depression of Europe was the seedbed of Hitler's militarism; his threats and his posturing were easily dismissed by Europeans who determined to accommodate him; Hitler had legitimate grievances, and out of these he built a formidable threat to the world.

In trying to sort this out, it occurred to me that I had never tried to love Adolf Hitler. From time to time I had tried to understand him and the forces that brought him to power. But love? Not by the longest stretch of the imagination.

The command to love our enemies, I decided at last, does not ask us to give them the moral high ground, or weaken our resolve to protect our fellow citizens. Loving our enemies is the sacrificial love that Jesus asked of us. Like so much else in the teaching and life of Jesus, it is a mystery, to be lived out even when it is not fully understood. Loving our enemies is a gift of grace.

To love our enemies, it is perhaps better to start small: not with bin Laden or Saddam Hussein, but with some adversary closer to home. We may be surrounded by difficult relationships, annoying associates, voices filled with criticism and spite. We can begin by forgiving them, trying to understand what is driving them, and praying for the grace to love them.

There are many passages in the Psalms where the psalmist prays to God for his enemies to be destroyed. But Jesus went beyond that and taught us, "For if you love those who love you, what reward do you have? And if you greet only your brothers and sisters, what more are you doing than others?" Jesus wanted us to stretch toward perfection. From the cross, in forgiving his own enemies, he made his teaching real and concrete.

The Easter *Triduum*, encompassing the three days of Holy Thursday, Good Friday, Holy Saturday, is an intense time of drawing close to Jesus in his death and resurrection. We sense that we can never entirely imitate his godly love. But we can break free of some of the boundaries that hold us captive. We can come closer to the light.

Be renewed in the spirit of your minds and . . . clothe your-self with the new self, created according to the likeness of God in true righteousness and holiness.

—Letter of Paul to the Ephesians

We do many things at Easter to proclaim our faith and our joy. We dress up. We decorate. We give gifts. We go to church. We affirm our baptismal promises. We sing. And we tell the resurrection stories: Mary Magdalene and the other disciples finding the empty tomb; Peter rushing into the empty tomb and finding the folded grave clothes; Mary Magdalene finding the risen Jesus and mistaking him for the gardener. We know these stories well, but we want to hear them again: the disciples walking with the risen Jesus on the Emmaus road; Jesus appearing to the disciples in the upper room, even when the door was closed; Thomas putting his fingers into Jesus' wounds and then, only then, affirming his faith in the risen Lord.

We hear the stories and we hear sermons about them. The ancient message is given again: Jesus has conquered death and shown us the resurrected life.

Sometimes we sit in church distractedly. The Easter lilies are so beautiful on the altar. The children look so cheerful in their Easter suits and dresses. Our thoughts turn to Easter baskets, Easter gatherings, Easter eggs. All these are signs of resurrected life. But our hearts want more.

To me it is clarifying to think that (as we read in Paul's letter to the Ephesians) that we are to "be renewed in the spirit of your minds and to clothe yourselves with the new self, created according to the likeness of God in true righteousness and holiness." Jesus is the next step in human transformation, and we are making that next step with him. One striking detail in many of the Resurrection stories is that Jesus came, but at first the disciples did not recognize him. No one fully understands what this means. At the very least, we assume that Jesus was changed in some way. However little we understand what happened on that first Easter, we can say this: Jesus rose—was raised—from death and showed himself to others and to us, to point us toward a next step, a definite transformation. He is transformed. And in him we also are being transformed.

Certain Scripture scholars draw a sharp line between the Jesus of history and the Christ of faith. They do this because the Resurrection stories are so remarkable. The resurrected Jesus has made a kind of quantum leap into a new kind of existence. Efforts to describe this existential leap fall short. Interpreters must resort to metaphors, saying the risen Jesus is on a higher plane, in a celestial realm. They say he has a transfigured identity, a glorified body. The old hymns and writings simply called it "glory." But the tie between the risen Jesus and the Jesus of history can't be broken. The Resurrection stories describe not an angel or a being of light, but a man named Jesus who at first was hard to recognize. The disciples knew him on the shore; they knew him in the upper room; they knew him in the breaking of the bread.

"Christ" is not a surname but a title. Jesus of Nazareth is called "Christ" (in Latin, *Christus;* in

Greek, *Christos*) because in Greek and Latin this word means "Messiah." Jesus is the Christ, the Messiah, the Anointed One. Jesus is Lord. Jesus is the Son of God.

Not many years after Jesus' death, resurrection, and ascension, Paul of Tarsus began to say in his writings that we are "in Christ." In Christ, he says, we are a new self and a new creation. We are in Christ and Christ is in us.

Sometimes we feel inadequate to being a new creation. We feel the handicap, the burden of our flawed humanity. But in Jesus, when we look attentively, we see the next step clearly. Paraphrasing St. Paul, C.S. Lewis writes in *Mere Christianity:* "In Christ a new kind of man has appeared, and the new life which began in him will be put into us."

What must we do to clothe ourselves with a new self? In fact, this is a work of grace, which seemingly comes over us when we are attentive, faithful, and believing. This is the reason for our rejoicing: that Jesus came for us and gave us the way to imitate him, to imitate God. However inadequate we may feel to this amazing destiny, it is ours; it is the promise that Jesus has made to us and lived out for us. Our task is to accept the grace, to make our small surrenders.

The three days of Easter are ending. The weeks that follow, from now to Pentecost, will continue our Easter celebration. Not only in these days, but every day, faith tells us our lives are being changed. We are becoming like Jesus, little Christs, moment by moment, Eucharist by Eucharist, day by day.

About the Author

Emilie Griffin has written and/or edited fifteen books on spiritual life, including *Turning* (about conversion), *Clinging* (about prayer), *The Reflective Executive* (about spirituality in the workplace), *Homeward Voyage: Reflections on Life-Changes, Wilderness Time: The Experience of Retreat,* and *Doors into Prayer.* She has collaborated with Richard Foster on an anthology, *Spiritual Classics in the Light of Twelve Spiritual Disciplines* (HarperCollins US, Winter 2000, and UK, October 1999). With Eugene Peterson she has co-edited *Epiphanies: Stories for the Christian Year.* Two of her titles have been published in Korean.

Emilie is a professional writer, editor, and marketing consultant. Her most recent titles are *Wonderful and Dark Is This Road: Discovering the Mystic Path,* and *Simple Ways to Pray: Spiritual*

Life in the Catholic Tradition. She is also the series editor of the *HarperCollins Spiritual Classics,* sixteen short works by devotional writers.

Griffin has worked extensively as a retreat and workshop leader. A member of the board of Renovaré, an infra-church movement committed to Christian renewal, she wrote a commentary on Proverbs for the *Renovaré Spiritual Formation Study Bible.* She has been a frequent contributor to *America: A Catholic Weekly.* On the Internet she has also contributed to "The High Calling" and "ExploreFaith."

A native of New Orleans and a Phi Beta Kappa graduate of Newcomb College, Tulane University, Emilie went to New York City as a *Mademoiselle* guest editor, and worked in New York in three major advertising agencies and on a special assignment for the Council of Better Business Bureaus.

Returning to New Orleans, she continued to work in major advertising and tourism firms and was named Advertising Copywriter of the Year by the Advertising Club of New Orleans. In all, she has won fifty awards for her creative work.

During her years in New York City she also studied playwriting with Edward Albee at the Circle in the Square Theater. Her first full-length play, *The Only Begotten Son*, won the First Playscript Prize from the Louisiana Council of Music and Performing Arts in 1971.

Emilie is married to William Griffin, a writer, editor, and publishing veteran who is an authority on C.S. Lewis and a translator of works by Augustine of Hippo and Thomas à Kempis. Both Griffins were founding members of the Chrysostom Society, a national writers group formed in the 1980s. Since 1998 they have lived in Alexandria, Louisiana.

Notes

viii *The Common Lectionary* *The Revised Common Lectionary* was introduced in 1994, and is used, with local translations, by the Roman Catholic Church and a number of Protestant churches. In the United States, this includes, among other churches, the Disciples of Christ, the Episcopal Church in the USA, the Evangelical Lutheran Church in America, the Presbyterian Church USA, the Reformed Church in America, the United Methodist Church, and the United Church of Christ. In the United Kingdom this includes the Church of England, the Methodist Church, the United Reformed Church, the Church in Wales, the Scottish Episcopal Church, and the Church of Scotland (Presbyterian).

3 *We are not converted . . . transformation in Christ* Thomas Merton, letter published in *Informations Catholiques Internationales*, April 1973, back cover.

4 *Then Jesus was led up . . . and afterwards he was famished* Matthew 4:1.

10 *Happy are those . . . whose hope is in the LORD their God* Psalm 146:5.

11   *the Son of Man must undergo great suffering . . .*
       Luke 9:22.

12   *Why then has this people turned away in perpetual back-*
       sliding?   Jeremiah 8:5.

16   *We are ever but beginning . . . as a hired servant*
       John Henry Newman, "On Christian Repentance,"
       in *Parochial and Plain Sermons,* vol. III, (London:
       Longmans Green, 1899), 90.

17   *If grace is so wonderful . . . unwelcome change*
       Kathleen Norris, "The Grace of Aridity and Other
       Comedies," in Philip Zaleski, ed., *The Best Spiritual*
       Writing 2004 (Boston: Houghton Mifflin, 2004).

21   *"You see, the older I get . . . living with God forever?"'*
       Brennan Manning, *A Glimpse of Jesus* (San Francisco:
       HarperSanFrancisco, 2003), 142.

25   *What then are we to say? . . . go on living in it?*
       Romans 6:1–2.

29   *It is no longer I who live . . . by faith in the Son of God*
       Galatians 2:20.

30   *Do not judge . . . and it will be given to you*   Luke 6:37–38.

35   *I . . . don't always have wonderful thoughts . . . is*
       greater than what I can grasp   Henri J.M. Nouwen,
       Spiritual Direction: Wisdom for the Long Walk of Faith
       (San Francisco: HarperSanFrancisco, 2006), 36.

40   *If you cannot go into the desert . . the stuff of your soul*
Carlo Carretto, *Letters from the Desert* (Maryknoll,
NY: Orbis Books, 2002), 67–68.

44   *It . . . is one of the most beautiful secrets of the spiritual life*
Carretto, *Letters from the Desert*, 46–47.

45   *We are responsible . . . to develop our own*   Henri J.M.
Nouwen, *The Way of the Heart: Desert Spirituality and
Contemporary Ministry* (New York: HarperCollins,
1991), 30.

49   *Everything contains some silence . . . a time when silence
reigned*   Kay Ryan, "Shark's Teeth," quoted in a
flyer from the Poetry Foundation, P.O. Box 575, Mt.
Morris, IL 61054.

50   *Yet even now . . . and relents from punishing*   Joel 2:12.

51   *The Golden String*   Bede Griffiths, *The Golden
String: An Autobiography* (Garden City, NY: Image
Books, 1964).

57   *Every walk is a story . . . and a time of reflection*   John
Leax, *Grace Is Where I Live* (LaPorte, IN: WordFarm,
2004), 113.

62   *God whispers . . . a deaf world*   C.S. Lewis, *The
Problem of Pain* (New York: Macmillan, 1975), 81.

65   *A thousand may fall . . . come near you*   Psalm 91:7.

66   *God wants our honest thoughts . . . not what we're supposed to say or feel*   Murray Bodo, OFM, *Poetry as Prayer: Denise Levertov* (Boston: Pauline Books & Media, 2001), 99.

67   *Abraham questions God about the people of Sodom* Genesis 18:22–33.

69   *Sacrifice and offering . . . written of me*   Psalm 40:6–7.

70   *The sacrifice acceptable to God . . . you will not despise* Psalm 51: 17.

71   *Certain vocations . . . provide a desert for reflection, a real monastery*   Ronald Rolheiser, *Forgotten Among the Lilies* (New York: Doubleday Galilee, 2005), 119.

74   *Let the little children come . . . it is to such as these that the kingdom of heaven belongs*   Matthew 19:14.

      Whoever does not receive the kingdom of God as a little child will never enter it   Mark 10:15.

75   *For a psychoanalyst . . . to study psychoanalysis in the first place*   J.D. Salinger, *Franny and Zooey* (Toronto/ NY: Bantam Books, 1964), 109.

78   *in your right hand are pleasures forevermore*   Psalm 16:11.

79   *Are we alert to the mercies that fill our days*   Kathy Coffey, *God in the Moment* (Maryknoll, NY: Orbis, 2005), 67.

83   *Sometimes there might be no words, but . . . you are in the process of praying*   Murray Bodo, OFM, *Poetry as Prayer: Denise Levertov*, 97.

89   *Pain and suffering are part and parcel . . . Christians are not exempt*   Philip Yancey, *Where Is God When It Hurts* (Grand Rapids, MI: Zondervan, 1977), 66.

Ask and you shall receive; knock and it shall be opened to you.   Paraphrase of Matthew 7:7.

90   *Father, I thank you . . . that they may believe that you sent me*   John 11:41b–42.

If your God is so terrific . . . it's so much more fun?   Paraphrase of Matthew 4:1–11.

94   *It is a good rule . . . reading old books*   C.S. Lewis, "On the Reading of Old Books," in *God in the Dock*, ed. Walter Hooper (Grand Rapids, MI: Eerdmans, 1970), 201–202.

96   *If we are truly docile . . . what can we do except trust him?*   Jean-Pierre de Caussade, *Abandonment to Divine Providence* (New York: Doubleday Image, 1975), 83.

98   *Finally, beloved . . . the God of peace will be with you*   Philippians 4:8–9.

99   *There are many slow days . . . when we aren't looking*   Eugene H. Peterson, *The Wisdom of Each Other* (Grand Rapids, MI: Zondervan, 1998), 57.

Be perfect, therefore, as your heavenly father is perfect   Matthew 5:48.

100   *I the LORD . . . fruit of their doings*   Jeremiah 17:10.

104   *Spiritual direction . . . the everydayness of your life is cultivated*   Peterson, *The Wisdom of Each Other*, 67.

107   *The slings and arrows . . . patient merit of the unworthy takes*   *Hamlet*, 3.1.

108   *You are my friends . . . I have heard from my Father*   John 15:14–15.

109   *When you get a problem . . . much the same*   Thomas à Kempis, *The Imitation of Christ*, trans. William Griffin (San Francisco: HarperSanFrancisco, 2000), 14.

110   *the woman who came with perfume in an alabaster jar*   Luke 7:36–39.

       Mary of Bethany anointing the feet of Jesus   John 12:3.

       the woman taken in adultery   John 8:2–11.

112   *Don't think about being good . . . that's all he wants at the moment*   Emilie Griffin, ed., *Evelyn Underhill: Essential Writings* (Maryknoll, NY: Orbis, 2003), 127. The other Underhill quotes in this reading are taken from this book.

116   *Blessed are those who trust . . . roots by the stream*   Jeremiah 17:7–8a.

119   *like a tree . . . leaves shall stay green*   Jeremiah 17:8.

123 *Our religion is not pure detachment . . . dance between the two*   Richard Rohr, *Everything Belongs* (New York: Crossroad, 1999, 2003), 170.

126 *no despair of ours . . . join in the general dance*   Thomas Merton, *New Seeds of Contemplation* (New York: New Directions, 1961), 296–97.

127 *The whole house . . . unbearable beauty of Christian life*   Letter from Evelyn Underhill to Baron Von Hugel, describing her retreat at Pleshey in 1922.

131 *For he will command his angels . . . dash your foot against a stone*   Psalm 91:11–12.

132 *We need a theology . . . [T]ime and grace wash clean*   Rolheiser, *Forgotten Among the Lilies*, 145.

133 *Believing there is no God means the suffering . . . isn't caused by an . . . omnipotent force*   Penn Jillette, *This I Believe*, National Public Radio broadcast, November 11, 2005.

134 *God is love, and those who abide in love abide in God, and God abides in them*   1 John 4:16b.

137 *So, when you are offering your gift . . . then come and offer your gift*   Matthew 5:23–24.

140 *You have heard . . . wants to borrow from you*   Matthew 5:38–42.

142 *She held up her hand . . . we survived*   Letter from

Jean Hardin to Emilie Griffin, March 2007.

Blessed are the merciful, for they will receive mercy Matthew 5:7.

143   *Then he will say . . . you did not do it to me*   Matthew 25:41–45.

Do not store up for yourselves treasures on earth . . . there will your heart be also   Matthew 6:19–21.

145   *Everyone then who hears these words . . . it had been founded on rock*   Matthew 7:24–25.

148   *Whenever you pray, do not be like the hypocrites* Matthew 6:5; *Whenever you fast, do not look dismal* Matthew 6:16; *When you give alms, do not let your left hand know what your right hand is doing* Matthew 6:3.

150   *Is this not the fast . . . from your own kin*   Isaiah 58:6–7.

152   *But now what do I do? . . . teach me your way of relinquishment*   Richard J. Foster, *Prayer: Finding the Heart's True Home* (San Francisco: HarperSanFrancisco, 1992), 56.

Blessed are the meek . . . inherit the earth   Matthew 5:5.

153   Excerpts from C.S. Lewis   C.S. Lewis, *Surprised by Joy* (New York: Harcourt, Brace & World, 1955), 224–25.

155 *Then he withdrew . . . not my will but yours be done*
Luke 22:42.

159 *I am the LORD . . . to give drink to my chosen people*
Isaiah 43:15, 19, 20.

161 *I never knew the man . . . I was never in Galilee* This
is my own paraphrase of Peter's denial as given in the
Gospels of Matthew, Mark, and Luke.

163 *I fled Him . . . down the arches of the years* Francis
Thompson, *The Hound of Heaven* (New York:
McCracken Press, 1993).

Francis Thompson (1859–1907).

168 *Our spiritual formation . . . born in human likeness*
Joshua Choonmin Kang, *Deep-Rooted in Christ:
The Way of Transformation* (Downers Grove, IL:
InterVarsity Press, 2007), 21.

172 *A moderate amount of anxiety . . . we would never
change* William A. Barry and William J. Connolly,
The Practice of Spiritual Direction (San Francisco:
HarperSanFrancisco, 1982), 85.

176 *But there are also many other . . . books that would be
written* John 21:25.

177 Dallas Willard, *The Divine Conspiracy* (San Francisco:
HarperSanFrancisco, 1998); *The Renovation of the
Heart* (Colorado Springs, CO: Navpress, 2002).

Eugene H. Peterson, *The Jesus Way* (Grand Rapids, MI: Eerdmans, 2007).

Gary Wills, *What Jesus Meant* (New York: Viking, 2006).

178   *But supposing that . . . I thought one could*   C.S. Lewis, in Walter Hooper, ed., *On Stories and Other Essays on Literature* (New York: Harcourt Brace Jovanovich, 1982), 47, in the essay "Sometimes Fairy Stories May Say Best What's to Be Said."

180   *When we suffer these things . . . putting our trust in God* Foster, *Prayer: Finding the Heart's True Home*, 223.

Woe to you . . . in sackcloth and ashes   Luke 10:13.

181   *How can this man give us his flesh to eat?*   John 6:52.

no longer went about with him   John 6:66.

Those who eat my flesh . . . will live for ever John 6:56, 58b.

Do you also wish to go away? . . . they would be faithful John 6:67–69.

Blessed are those who are persecuted . . . Rejoice and be glad Matthew 5:10–12.

182   *Whenever you face trials . . . brings us to full maturity* James 1:2–4.

185   *The Christian religion asks ... in our ordinary circumstances*
Kathleen Norris, *The Quotidian Mysteries: Laundry,
Liturgy and Women's Work* (New York: Paulist Press,
1998), 77–78.

186   Thérèse Martin (1873–1897).

193   *The pilgrims covered ... the destiny of Israel*
Robert Aron, *The Jewish Jesus* (Maryknoll, NY: Orbis
Books, 1971), 97.

194   *every Jewish male was obligated to go to the temple three times
a year*   See Exodus 23:14 and Deuteronomy 16:16.

       They were on the road ... what was to happen to him
Mark 10:32.

198   *Christ is still a pilgrim ... already in the Heart of Destiny*
Paul Marechal, *Dancing Madly Backwards* (New
York: Crossroad, 1982), 25.

200   *In him a new age has dawned ... man is once again
made whole*   Easter Preface IV, from the Liturgy of
the Mass. The reference is to Jesus Christ.

201   *Jesus was another pilgrim . . . every place his home*
Marechal, *Dancing Madly Backwards*, 25.

       Where I am going . . . you will follow afterward
John 13:36.

203   *Then he said to them ... follow me*   Luke 9:23.

205 Henry Vaughan (1622–1695) was a Christian mystical poet.

206 *Six days later . . . talking with him*   Matthew 17:1–3.

Tell no one . . . raised from the dead   Matthew 17:9.

208 Gerard Manley Hopkins, *The Wreck of the Deutschland*, in *Gerard Manley Hopkins: Poems and Prose* (London, Penguin Books, 1953), 24.

213 *The Eucharist is . . . a present reality in our midst* Joseph Cardinal Ratzinger (Pope Benedict XVI), *God Is Near Us: The Eucharist the Heart of Life* (San Francisco: Ignatius Press, 2003), 44.

214 *Peter said to him . . . also my hands and my head*   John 13:8–9.

216 *While they were eating . . . in my Father's kingdom* Matthew 26:26–29.

219 *Could I behold those hands . . . pierced with those holes* John Donne, "Good Friday 1613: Riding Westward," in Herbert Grierson, ed., *The Poems of John Donne* (London: Oxford University Press, 1960), 306.

220 *Destroy this temple . . . I will raise it up*   John 2:19.

222 *If we have learned . . . with his eyes*   Avery Cardinal Dulles, "Love, the Pope and C.S. Lewis," *First Things*, January 2007.

225 *For if you love...stretch toward perfection* Matthew 5:46–48.

227 *Be renewed . . . in true righteousness and holiness* Ephesians 4:23–24.

Mary Magdalene and the other disciples finding the empty tomb Matthew 28:1; Mark 16:1.

Peter rushing into the empty tomb and finding the folded grave clothes Luke 24:12.

Mary Magdalene finding the risen Jesus and mistaking him for the gardener John 20:1–18.

the disciples walking with the risen Jesus on the Emmaus road Luke 24:13–32.

Jesus appearing to the disciples in the upper room, even when the door was closed John 20:19–21.

Thomas putting his fingers into Jesus' wounds and . . . affirming his faith in the risen Lord John 20:24–29.

228 *be renewed . . . in true righteousness and holiness* Ephesians 4:23–24.

230 *we are a new self* Colossians 3:10.

a new creation Galatians 6:15.

In Christ a new kind of man...put into us C.S. Lewis, *Mere Christianity* (San Francisco: HarperSanFrancisco, 2001), 60.

About Paraclete Press

Who We Are

Paraclete Press is a publisher of books, recordings, and DVDs on Christian spirituality. Our publishing represents a full expression of Christian belief and practice—from Catholic to Evangelical, from Protestant to Orthodox.

We are the publishing arm of the Community of Jesus, an ecumenical monastic community in the Benedictine tradition. As such, we are uniquely positioned in the marketplace without connection to a large corporation and with informal relationships to many branches and denominations of faith.

What We Are Doing

Books—Paraclete publishes books that show the richness and depth of what it means to be Christian. Although Benedictine spirituality is at the heart of all that we do, we publish books that reflect the Christian experience across many cultures, time periods, and houses of worship. We publish books that nourish the vibrant life of the church and its people—books about spiritual practice, formation, history, ideas, and customs.

We have several different series, including the best-selling Living Library, Paraclete Essentials, and Paraclete Giants series of classic texts in contemporary English; A Voice from the Monastery—men and women monastics writing about living a spiritual life today; award-winning literary faith fiction and poetry; and the Active Prayer Series that brings creativity and liveliness to any life of prayer.

Recordings—From Gregorian chant to contemporary American choral works, our music recordings celebrate sacred choral music through the centuries. Paraclete distributes the recordings of the internationally acclaimed choir Gloriæ Dei Cantores, praised for their "rapt and fathomless spiritual intensity" by *American Record Guide*, and the Gloriæ Dei Cantores Schola, which specializes in the study and performance of Gregorian chant. Paraclete is also the exclusive North American distributor of the recordings of the Monastic Choir of St. Peter's Abbey in Solesmes, France, long considered to be a leading authority on Gregorian chant.

DVDs—Our DVDs offer spiritual help, healing and biblical guidance for life issues: grief and loss, marriage, forgiveness, anger management, facing death, and spiritual formation.

Learn more about us at our Web site:
www.paracletepress.com, or call us toll-free at
1-800-451-5006.

You May Also Enjoy . . .

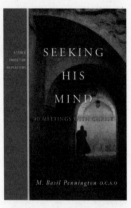

Seeking His Mind
M. Basil Pennington, ocso

ISBN: 978-1-55725-562-4
$15.95, Trade paper

Beloved spiritual teacher Basil Pennington shares the fruits of his many years of *lectio divina*, an ancient method of hearing and meditating on the word of God. Presented in forty daily readings, each meditation is inspired by a Scripture verse from the life and teachings of Christ.

Available at bookstores
or online at www.paracletepress.com

You May Also Enjoy ...

Doors Into Prayer
Emilie Griffin

ISBN: 978-1-55725-456-6
$12.95, Trade paper

Whether you are a beginner at prayer or further along in the journey, this little book will offer profound wisdom and encouragement. With a spirit of warmth and simplicity, Emilie Griffin offers helpful insights on the many ways to pray, overcoming discouragement and doubt, and the possibilities of prayer.

Available at bookstores
or online at www.paracletepress.com